Garfield Robinson

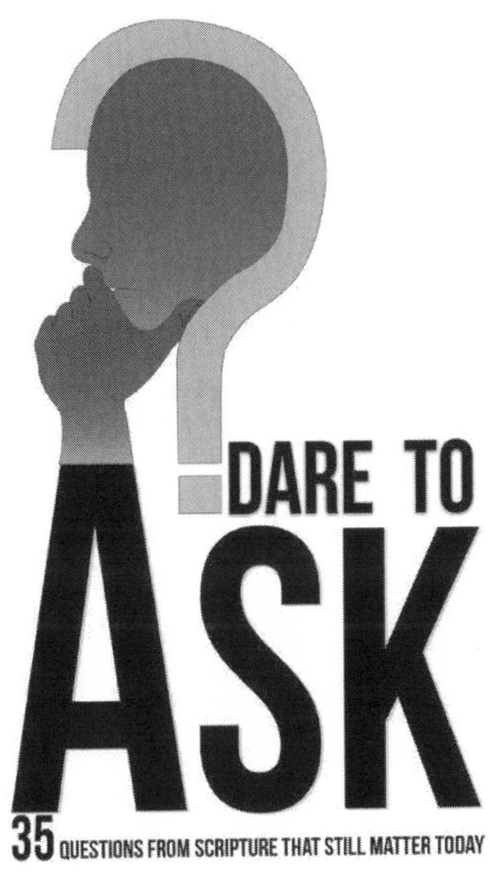

Extra MILE Innovators
Kingston, Jamaica W.I.

**ISBN:** 978-1-62676-483-5



. . . . .

Published by:
Extra MILE Innovators
21 Phoenix Avenue,
Kingston 10, Jamaica W.I.
www.extramileja.com

Edited by Extra MILE Innovators
Cover Designer: Albert Burkett
origmullob@yahoo.com

**Author Contact**

For consultation, feedback or speaking engagements, contact the author at
robinsongarfield15@gmail.com

Scripture References

Scripture quotations marked (ESV)are taken from THE HOLY BIBLE, ENGLISH STANDARD VERSION, ESV® Text Edition: 2016. Copyright © 2001 by Crossway Bibles, a publishing ministry of Good News Publishers.

Scripture quotations identified (KJV) are from the KING JAMES VERSION OF THE BIBLE (Public Domain).

Scripture quotations marked (NIV) are from the HOLY BIBLE, NEW INTERNATIONAL VERSION; copyright © 1973, 1978, 1984, 2010 by the International Bible Society, and Biblica, Inc.™ Used by permission. All rights reserved worldwide.

**Dare to Ask Bonus Chapter**

Request your bonus chapter with three additional questions at
https://forms.gle/xqBr66eHMvP9FbeS6

# Dedication

*This book is gratefully dedicated to the special ladies in my life. First and foremost, my wife, Marlene, who has always been there for me, a shoulder to lean on, and the wind beneath my wings.*

*To my mom, Cindy, for her constant support, and my three daughters, Kadian, Shantelle and Breanne for their encouragement along the journey.*

# Praise for the Book

In this very relevant work, Robinson encourages readers to "Dare to Ask." His easy-going manner tackles questions that arise from well-known Bible passages and provides well-reasoned answers anchored in the passages themselves instead of speculation often common in such matters. He covers a wide breadth of passages and issues that will bring the thoughtful reader much delight. I heartily endorse this work.

—David Pearson
Former Academic Dean
Jamaica Theological Seminary

. . . . . . . . .

Yes, like his Lord and Master, the writer of this masterpiece—Garfield Robinson—is a friend of sinners. Both sinners and saints will benefit from this book. Why? Because it poses some of the best questions ever aired and proffers some very good answers to these queries. It was the late great Johnny Nash who sang the bestselling single: 'There Are More Questions than Answers'; the writer of this thought-provoking literary gem wisely focuses our attention on Jesus; the only person who has all the answers.

In the possession of an anti-Christ, a question can be used as a weapon leading to destruction, as we see in Genesis 3. But on the lips of someone interested in human flourishing to the glory of God, any question is a pedagogical tool for personal advancement. This book undoubtedly falls in the latter category. Even the all-knowing God employs what we may call the rhetoric of interrogation.

How we answer such a God may reveal the deceitfulness of our heart. For example, Adam blamed his sin on Eve and God when God asked him "Where are you?" The best thing about this book is that the answers are drawn from the best Source—the Source of light and the Source of life. The only thing I don't like about the project is that I wish it were given to me. Oops! I think I'm hearing a voice whispering: 'What is that to you?' When you are through reading, I believe you will in the final analysis agree that a Part 2 is justified. And Garfield, thanks for the privilege and honour.

—Dr. Delano Palmer
Former Deputy President, Jamaica Theological
Seminary (JTS),
Life-Time Member,
Christian Ambassadors Footballers United (CAFU)

. . . . . . . . . .

As humans, we constantly search for knowledge, clarification, for answers to life's questions. Confusion is often created because of the varying answers we receive to many of our questions. This is often true in relation to biblical questions.

Against this background, I believe, the writer has carefully selected questions that are often asked by persons searching for truth and compiled them in one place for easy access. The answers seem to facilitate hope in, and assurance of faith in God. The answers inform and challenge readers to examine personal beliefs and practices. Any reader in his quest for spiritual growth and strengthened faith in God, will find useful nuggets in this book. This book is for Christians and non-Christians as some of these unanswered questions are what delays the unsaved from making a commitment to follow Christ.

If you are at all desirous of growing in your faith and trust in the supreme God, then this book is absolutely essential to have. It can be used as a devotional as you focus on the questions and carefully absorb them. Do not rush through, but spend time and allow the Word to dwell in you richly.

I believe this book can also be used as a tool for Bible Study and rich discussion. This material is engaging and life changing, Kudos to the writer for his insight and careful explanation. It is a must have for Christians, bible teacher and for those who mentor and disciple others.

—Dr. Hyacinth Peart
Family Counsellor

# Foreword

Garfield Robinson is a student of the Word. He is committed to, and participates in many social activities. Many of us know of his loves: family, football, food! But, his passion is the Word. He embraces its candor, complexity, clarity. He lives by the Word. His excitement when he is handling the Word, whether preaching or teaching is palpable.

Pastor, as a diligent student, knows that questions are often more important than answers. Questions open up wide vistas to explore issues, engage others in a process of mutual learning, expose ignorance, establish options, encourage us to challenge assumptions, and allow us the privilege of acknowledging that there are moments when we just don't know.

Answers provide contextual and time-bound responses that have their place. Answers without interrogation suggest certitude. We know! Yes, there are times that we Know! But, in engaging others in conversations about life, when answers are provided without authentic questioning, persons either follow blindly or without passion.

The Word is both text and person. Bible and Jesus. Both demand that we engage in thoughtful conversations. Through *Dare to Ask* Garfield invites us to consider both from a fresh perspective. Yes, he deals with issues for which answers are often assumed: love, forgiveness, anger, family, care for others, grace in response to sin, abandonment, trust, anxiety, eternity. Garfield knows that the questions that he explores help us to appreciate the Word.

He applies his inquisitive hermeneutics to tease issues and principles for our consideration. Many of the passages are familiar to us. The discussion may not be. The issues that *Dare to Ask* highlights are central to our ability to experience God in wholesome ways. The Bible provides us with the lived experiences of many persons and groups who grappled with issues that we still face as human beings. *Dare to Ask* is a useful and practical illustration of these issues, the questions used to engage people, how the persons in the situations responded, and the eternal lessons. The lessons, yes, the answers, however have to be applied in our lived experiences. How? **Dare to Ask!**

—Dr. Dameon Black
Former Principal,
Jamaica Theological Seminary (JTS)

# Table of Contents

# Introduction

I heard of a man who was in his living room and he wanted to get on to the computer, so he yelled "honey what's the password for the computer." She shouted, "It's the date of our anniversary" the man became disappointed and sad because he did not remember the date he got married, and he was too ashamed to ask her. Some people like to ask questions even though they may not like the answers. Some are afraid or ashamed to ask questions because they believe others will look down on them for asking. But questions are very important, and they play a significant role in human relationship and development.

Asking questions help us to deal with the concerns we are faced with and offer solutions to treat the problems. Getting good answers is the main course of increasing our knowledge and improving our intellect. In this book, we seek to answer many questions that are asked in Scripture, that people today are curious about. We also offer insight into how to deal with some psychological, emotional, social and spiritual matters in a biblical way. There are so many people who are haunted by questions of origin, purpose, and destiny. They ask, "Who am I?" "Why am I here?" "Where am I going?" The Bible answers all these questions and many more.

In my 28 years as a Bible teacher, I've never seen a time that is more urgent to have sound biblical answers for those who are searching. This book will bring about transformation in the lives of those who put the information into action. This is not a book to be read all at once. It's for contemplation and introspection. My hope for everyone who reads this book is that they may engage with Scripture in a more purposeful way, and that their personal intimacy with Jesus will get sweeter as the days go by. Remember that God is already perfect therefore He cannot get any better than He is right now, but our relationship with Him can get better. I also hope that at the end of each presentation, you will consider the questions to ponder and to discuss. This is an excellent tool for Bible teachers to use as conversation starters and group discussion.

# PART 1:
# DEALING WITH ANGER AND JEALOUSY

# 1.

# What is going on?

## —Luke 15:26 (NIV)

## Put Away Your Anger

I once heard about a boy who rebelled against his father and left home. He stayed away for a very long time but later began longing for home. He was not sure if his father still loved him or whether he would accept him back, so he wrote him a letter. The letter reads: "Dad I want to come home, if you are willing to welcome me back, please leave a white shirt on the line so I will know if I should get off the train and come home." When the boy arrived, he was greeted with love and forgiveness. He then said to his father "Dad, I believe all the homes on this road welcome home a son today because from the train I could see a white shirt on every line." The father smiled and said, "Son you've been away for so long and I did not want you to miss my answer by missing the shirt on the line, so I asked the people if they would allow me to place a shirt on their line. I wanted you to know that the answer is yes, a thousand times yes."

There is a similar story of a lost son in Luke 15:11-32. After Jesus finished talking about the lost sheep and the lost coin, He spoke of a lost son. One day the son came to his father and requested that his father give him what was going to be his inheritance (v12). This was [a bit] inappropriate for the youngster to do; however, the father obliged him and gave him the allotment (v12). The young man wanted to live independently of his father. He wanted his own space, his own time, his own friends and his own finances. Is this a picture of how we are sometimes when we want to do what we want in the way we want to do it? He imagined how good it would be if he could be in full control of his life without anyone telling him what to do. He was not willing to humble himself even to the Almighty God? He wasted his wealth with a vain lifestyle and squandered his substance recklessly (v13).

His friends left him and he was now broke having no one to give him anything (vv14-16). We know that when he went away from his father and from his family that this was a serious misjudgment on his part. The good thing about this young man, though, is that he came to his senses (v17). It happened when he was at the lowest point in his life, when he was thinking of doing things that ordinarily he would not do. For example, he wanted the food that the pigs were eating (v 16). He reached a very low point in his mind and his desires, but he came to his senses, got up out of the pig pen, and went home. We see something interesting in the story, that being away from the father is not as sweet as it seems at first (v 17-18). It was the love and the care of his father that drew him back. Sometimes we don't realize what we have until we lose it. Whenever we leave our Heavenly Father, we enter a spiritual famine. This is true even of people who stay in church but don't have intimate fellowship with their heavenly Father.

The boy repented and returned to his father. Now look at the response of his father: he loved him and embraced him and welcomed him home (vv. 20-24). Remember that home is where the father is. The father ordered his servants to make preparation for a celebration (v. 22).

When the elder son came from working in the field, he inquired of the servants, "**What is going on?" (v26, NIV)** The servant told him that his father was celebrating the return of his younger brother. The elder son became angry and would not go inside.

There are some important lessons for us to learn right here. Notice that there was no favoritism or partiality with the father, just as he went out to his younger son (v 20), he also went out to his elder son v 28). We, too, must love our children equally even though that love may be expressed or applied differently.

The elder son displayed an unforgiving and judgmental attitude. Yes, the younger son had left the family, but the father forgave him. And yes, he squandered his inheritance, but the father has received him back. The boy was not trying to get more of his father's wealth or legacy, he just wanted to come home. But the other son did not want him home. Maybe because he wanted the estate or maybe because he knew that the father would show his brother the same amount of love and affection as he did before he left and maybe he thought that his younger brother who had rebelled didn't deserve the father's love and forgiveness.

But none of us deserves forgiveness. Both sons needed to learn a lesson on grace that day. The truth is that grace is not earned nor deserved. Grace is a one-way thing. It's from the giver to the receiver. The younger son did not realize that he did not become a son by doing good works and the elder son thought that he deserved to be a son because of his good works. Notice how the elder son pointed to his perfect record. He said, "I have never disobeyed your command" (v 29). He then straightway accused his father of not being fair when he said "Yet you never gave me a young goat, that I might celebrate with my friends" (v 29). He obviously did not know his father well because he had lived with and around his father and yet did not really know him.

This is also true of some people who will never stop coming to church, but they have stopped coming to God. They refuse to walk away from church, but they have walked away from Christ long ago. The father said to the elder son, "All that is mine is yours" (v 31). This means that he could have taken a goat whenever he wanted.

In several verses we see the younger son's repentance demonstrated (v 17-21). We also see an illustration of the father's loving response to his children (v 22-24, 28, 31-32). However, the elder son had a different attitude. Let us look closer at the elder son's rebellion and resistance towards his father. When the father realized that the elder son refused to come into the party, he went out to him. He pleaded with him over and over to come in, but the son refused to listen. He disowned his brother by stating "when this your son has returned, you kill the fatted calf" (v30).

When we disown our brother, we also deny our father. If we despise and disown a child of our Heavenly Father, he is still our brother. So why must we celebrate the brother who has returned? Firstly, we should join the party because we too have fallen, we too have sinned. None of us is perfect. It might be a different sin, but it still hurts the Father.

Secondly, we must join the celebration because heaven rejoices for the one that has returned. "Just so, I tell you, there is joy before the angels of God over one sinner who repents" (Luke 15:10). Thirdly, we should join the celebration because it is fitting, it is the right thing to do. Fourthly, we should celebrate because others will be able to witness a redemptive community of people who are willing to give grace to others because they too have received grace. The fact that we have freely received mercy, love and grace from our **Heavenly Father** requires we must freely give love and grace to others. This will serve as a great attraction to the Christian faith and to God himself. So let us put away our anger and seek to be more compassionate towards those who have strayed from the right path. They need us now even more than before.

## Additional Questions to Ponder/Discuss

a. Has love ever brought you home?
b. How far away did you go from the Father?
c. What specific thing about God caused you to come home?
d. What is the most important lesson that you learned?
e. Why was the elder brother so angry?

# 2.

# Do you do well to be angry?

## —Jonah 4:4

## When We Miss God's Agenda

The story about the prophet Jonah and his response to God is a very intriguing one. The people of Nineveh were very wicked and immoral. God sent Jonah to preach and warn them that if they did not repent, He was going to destroy them. Here is where the story gets interesting. Jonah knew that if the people repented, then God would relent; so, he decided to run away from the mission to which God had called him because as far as he was concerned the Ninevites did not deserve forgiveness.

Although Jonah believed strongly that the Ninevites didn't deserve forgiveness, he did not seem to understand that no one does. This was a fundamental flaw in Jonah's understanding of grace and forgiveness. He considered himself worthy of mercy because he was not as wicked as the Ninevites. Mercy and grace are not earned nor deserved, they are gifts given freely and received freely.

Jonah was so angry at God for the grace given to Nineveh that he wanted to die. When a believer reaches such a state of hatred and bitterness, s/he becomes so blinded that s/he cannot see the beauty of God's grace. God wanted to teach Jonah a lesson with the hope of bringing him to his senses.

However, it is evident that no message from God was going to change his conviction. God showed him mercy by sparing his life when he was thrown from the ship and was inside the belly of the great fish. God also provided shelter from the heat that was scorching on him. When God destroyed the tree that sheltered him, he was hurt because he had concern for it, but he had no care if God destroyed the thousands of people in the city.

Sometimes we can get caught up in caring only for things that matter to us and things that bring us personal comfort. As believers, we should take note of what matters to God, because those things should also matter to us. Is there someone that you dislike, so much so that it would hurt you if God saved him? Are you more concerned about your friends or family and personal comfort than doing the work that brings God pleasure? Remember God will have mercy on those who show mercy.

God asked Jonah the same question twice. Let us look at the question. God did not ask if it felt nice to be angry or if he liked to be angry; instead, God asked, **"Do you do well to be angry?" (Jonah 4:4)** This is a question we all need to answer as we look at other people who seem to be graced far more than we are. Is it right for us to be angry? It is quite fitting for us to be angry about some things, such as wrong deeds or sin, but in our anger, we must not sin (Ephesians 4:26).

What is worthy of note in this situation is that the prophet was not angry about sin and sinners. He was angry at God and His grace. There is nothing bad about having a God who is merciful and slow to anger, one who is not willing that any should perish, but that all should come to repentance (2 Peter 3:9). Is it right for you to be angry or should you thank Him and be happy? This story ended with Jonah being angry at God and with his clenched fist and a bitter heart. I trust that our story will end with us shouting, "Thy will be done Lord!"

## Additional Questions to Ponder/Discuss

a. What did you learn from how God treated Jonah?
b. Is it the degree of the pain that determines your forgiveness of others?
c. Why did Jonah want all those people dead?
d. Did Jonah have a right to be angry?
e. Would you be angry at God if he saves someone you don't like?

# 3.

# Am I my brother's keeper?

## —Genesis 4:9

## Helping My Brother

Have you ever watched a bunch of crabs in a barrel? I have seen it before. It was funny at first just watching the crabs stepping on each other to get to the top of the barrel. They pull down the crab that is ahead of them so none can make it to the top. The longer I watched, the less amusing it became. Although I was not in that barrel, I could only imagine the frustration of the crabs that were there. However, these are just crabs, they don't know any better. Isn't it sad when people behave the same as these crabs?

It is a fact, that when we hold on to grudges it will have a negative ripple effect on our intimacy with God, our social relationship with others and it will even affect the way we relate to ourselves. This is one of the reasons why we are admonished in Scripture to forgive quickly, even when we have a legitimate reason to be angry. In Ephesians 4:26-27 we are told, "Be angry and do not sin; do not let the sun go down on your anger, and give no opportunity to the devil." When we refuse to forgive, we set up ourselves for failure and for deception by the devil.

Sometimes the offender is not even aware that they did or said something that hurt you. In the story we are about to look at, we see no evidence that Abel did anything wrong to be at the receiving end of such hatred from his brother. All we see in the text is that there was great jealousy towards Abel.

Let us examine the story and see the destructive domino effect that holding a grudge has. It caused a severe erosion on the fabric of their relationships. Their parents would have been hurt because they lost their two sons. They lost Abel to murder, and Cain because God judged him and sent him away as punishment for the killing of his brother.

In the book of Genesis, God asked Cain a question and instead of answering the question, Cain asked God a question. Let us look at what was happening in this situation. Cain had just killed his brother Abel, and God confronted him about his sin. Instead of confessing and repenting, he responded with an attitude of rebellion and pride. Here is where we find Cain's question: "Am I my brother's keeper?" (Genesis 4:9)

Cain thought he had the power to do as he liked. His attitude also showed that he did not think that he was accountable to anyone for his action. If he was not pleased with his circumstances, then he felt he was free to do whatever he desired to get out of the situation. Cain was jealous of his brother, not because of what Abel had done, but because of how God was working in his brother's life, and the fact that God was pleased with him (Genesis 4:4).

Sometimes people become jealous and bitter against others not because of any wrong they have done, but because it seems like the blessings of the Lord are on them. That shows that Cain neglected his responsibility to help his brother. Instead of seeking harmony with his brother and helping him, he chose to hurt his brother (Genesis 4:6-8).

Are you your brother's/sister's keeper? Are you looking out for his/her interests or well-being? If we allow jealousy to remain in our hearts, we could find ourselves responding in anger towards others like Cain did with his brother Abel.

God was not showing favoritism towards Abel. Abel simply did that which was right, and it was pleasing to God. According to Hebrews 11, it was by his faith that Abel offered a more acceptable offering than Cain. This is why the writer of Hebrews says God accepted his gift and referred to him as righteous (Hebrews 11:4).

Don't allow low self-esteem or low achievement to cause you to hurt others. Seek help to deal with the hurt you are experiencing. Remember that hurting people usually hurt people, so get help in order to give help. Cain did not give help to his brother because he rejected the counsel God gave him while he was angry and hurting. According to Genesis 4:6, "The Lord said to Cain, why are you angry, and why has your face fallen? If you do well, will you not be accepted?

And if you do not well, sin is crouching at the door. Its desire is for you but you must rule over it."

Don't be blinded by your pain to the extent that you start fighting people who are not at war with you. Sin has a way of creeping up on us instead of leaping on us. It often takes us by surprise when we recognize how dark our hearts have become. Cain found himself in a similar situation where he lost control of himself.

The Bible tells us that Cain killed his brother Abel while they were out in the field (Genesis 4:10). Can you imagine him talking to his brother and then striking him dead? I don't know how long Cain had been carrying around that anger and bitterness against his brother. The Bible doesn't tell us. But what it does tell us, is that God saw that he was struggling with these feelings and warned him that sin is at his door waiting to destroy him. This is why we need to quickly deal with any root of bitterness, resentment or hatred towards others.

If at that time Cain had released his hatred against his brother he would not have been tricked and trapped by Satan. If we love God whom we cannot see, we ought to love those we can see. If we truly love, we will also seek to forgive. In 1 Corinthians 13:4-7 we read

> "Love is patient and kind; love does not envy or boast; it is not arrogant or rude. It does not insist on its own way; it is not irritable or resentful; it does not rejoice at wrongdoing, but rejoices with the truth. Love bears

all things, believes all things, hopes all things endures all things."

God takes note of those whose lives are snuffed out; He knows those who are carrying out these evil acts and He will call them into account. In Genesis 4:10 it says "And the Lord said, what have you done? The voice of your brother's blood is crying out to me from the ground"

He was calling Cain to take responsibility for what he had done. He wanted Cain to acknowledge his sinful act and repent, but Cain refused to repent. God then laid out the consequence of Cain's sin while still showing him mercy (Genesis 4:11-15)

There are several Scriptures that tell us that we will give an account to God for the deeds done in our body (Romans 14:12; 2 Corinthians 5:10; Romans 2:6-8). Those who seek to do evil and ruin people's lives will stand in judgment before God. Knowing that we will all give an account for the way we live, how will we answer the following questions? Are you willing to run the risk of having negative effects that destroy your relationships and your intimacy with God by holding a grudge and refusing to forgive? Is it worth it? If your answer to these questions is no, then it is time to forgive.

## Additional Questions to Ponder/Discuss

a. How could Cain have avoided killing his brother?
b. Do you feel a little jealous when someone around you gets blessed?

c. List two things that can follow when we hold grudges?
d. Do you feel a sense of accountability for your brethren?
e. Does knowing that God sees everything impact your behaviour?

# PART 2
# DEALING WITH JESUS AND SALVATION

# 4.

# Where is the Lamb for the offering? —Genesis 22:7

## The Lamb Really Came

Have you ever been in a class and the teacher is saying something that you can see where it works up to a point, but you need more information? There may be others who are in a similar situation where they need further clarification, but they are afraid to ask the question. Isaac, on this occasion was not afraid to ask the question, "Where is the lamb for the burned offering?" God had made a promise to Abraham that through Isaac His covenant would be fulfilled (Genesis 21:12). This is primarily in reference to Jesus through whom salvation would come to the whole world (Galatians 3:7-9). The ultimate promise is that salvation will be provided through Abraham's seed which is Jesus. "Now the promises were made to Abraham and to his offspring. It does not say, "And to offsprings," referring to many, but referring to one, "And to your offspring," who is Christ (Galatians 3:16 ).

There was a picture given of the substitutionary death of Christ in this story. This is seen in the ram/lamb that was slain. Abraham said to Isaac, "God will provide for himself the lamb." Isn't that wonderful to hear that the ram/lamb that was slain that day was a picture of the lamb that would be slain on mount Calvary centuries later? The Scriptures tell us that one day, John pointed to Jesus and said, "Behold the Lamb of God who takes away the sins of the world" (John 1:29).

In the book of Isaiah, we read that the lamb was crushed, chastised for our sins, he bore our griefs and carried our sorrows (Isaiah 53:4-5). This is what brought peace and hope to the world. In the same way Abraham told his servants that he and Isaac were going to worship and return (Genesis 22:5). Jesus told his servants that He was about to do His act of worship through obedience to the Father and submission to His will and then He would return.

Abraham did not know exactly how God was going to fulfil His promise, but he knew that God would. We are told in the book of Hebrews that Abraham trusted God's faithfulness to His word, that he was prepared to receive Isaac from the dead. He was convinced that God was able to raise Isaac so as to fulfill his promise (Hebrews 11:17-19). The text goes on to say that Abraham received Isaac from the dead figuratively. This is so because Abraham considered Isaac given or offered to God. It was a done deal in his heart.

So, this is like receiving him back from the dead. This is a very important point because Abraham made a commitment to God and he did not allow anything to change his mind. With all the pain that his commitment brought, he remained steadfast and focused on seeing God's will be done.

We get a picture of this in the garden when we hear Jesus agonizing over what He was about to do. Nevertheless, he said, "My Father, if it be possible let this cup pass from me; nevertheless, not as I will but as you will" (Matthew 26:39). The Lord had promised that the Seed of the woman would crush the head of the serpent. Please note that this was pointing to Jesus at Calvary where He crushed Satan's head and Satan bruised his heel. Although Jesus was hurt in the battle, He ultimately won the war. Jesus has broken the hopeless sequence of birth, life and then death. In Genesis chapter 5 we read that they were born, they lived and they died, but with Jesus, we can have eternal life because He rose from the grave. For us who are born in the sequence of birth, life and death, Jesus makes the difference that gives hope to the world.

## Additional Questions to Ponder/Discuss

a. Why was Jesus called the Lamb of God?
b. Why was it necessary for Jesus to be our substitute?
c. Could Jesus have paid for our sins without dying?

d. Why did Abraham tell his servants that he and his will come back?
e. Why did God declare Abraham righteous?

# 5.

# Who do you say I am?

### Matthew 16:15

## Knowing Jesus Really Matters

In Matthew 16:13-16 Jesus tested his disciples by asking them some questions. He first asked them

> 'Who do people say that the Son of man is?' And they said, "Some say John the Baptist, others say Elijah, and others Jeremiah or one of the prophets." He said to them, "But who do you say that I am?" Simon Peter replied, "You are the Christ, the Son of the living God."

Jesus asked a couple questions in the passage that we want to look at.

> Now when Jesus came into the district of Caesarea Philippi, he asked his disciples, "Who do people say that the Son of Man is?" And they said, "Some say John the Baptist, others say Elijah, and others Jeremiah or one of the prophets." He said to them, "But who do you say that I am?" Simon Peter replied, "You are the Christ, the Son of the living God." And Jesus answered him, "Blessed are you, Simon Bar-Jonah! For flesh and blood has not revealed this to you, but my Father who is in heaven. And I tell you, you are Peter, and on this rock[b] I will build my church, and the gates of hell[c] shall not prevail against it. I will give you the keys of the kingdom of heaven, and whatever you bind on earth shall be bound in heaven, and whatever you loose on earth shall be loosed[d] in heaven." Then he strictly charged the disciples to tell no one that he was the Christ (Matthew 16: 20).

The first is the question about who people say Jesus is. In that time many persons were seeing and hearing about Jesus, but they still did not know who He was. Some said that He was John the Baptist, others said Elijah. Some said Jeremiah, others just thought that He was a prophet. Today we hear some similar responses to the question of who Jesus is. Some say He was a prophet, others say he was just a good man, while others believe that he was a lunatic.

Many people spoke evil of Jesus then and we find many are speaking evil of Him now. Author C.S Lewis makes a profound statement in his book "Mere Christianity" when he warned us not to make the mistake of calling Jesus just a good man. He says that there are three options: either Jesus is a liar, and therefore we don't need to believe His claims; or He is a lunatic, and therefore we need not take Him seriously; or He is indeed Lord, and we need to bow down and worship Him. The option of "good man" is not open to us, if Jesus is who He claims or Jesus is worse than a liar or a lunatic. This is why it is so important that we know who Jesus is.

This brings us to the second question Jesus asked the disciples, "Who do you say I am?" We need to know what people have to say about who Jesus is. But it can do us more harm than good if we don't know the truth of who Jesus is for ourselves. For example, there are some groups who will affirm that Jesus is good but they will not refer to Him as God. Some say that He is just a man who became God and therefore we can do the same. These groups are not trusting in Jesus as their only hope for salvation. The Scripture reminds us in Acts 4:12 "And there is salvation in no one else, for there is no other name under heaven given among men by which we must be saved".

Saul was a dedicated Pharisee who was very zealous for the law in Judaism. So, he sought to persecute, imprison and even kill people who were believers in Jesus. But one day while he was on his journey the Lord struck him from his horse and he became blind. Saul then asked a very important question of the Lord who spoke to him from heaven. The question was, "Who are you, Lord?" The Lord answered and said, "I am Jesus." (Acts 9:5) Saul was sincere in his drive to destroy the Christians because he thought that he was doing God's will. However, as we found out, he was wrong. It is important to note that people who are sincere in what they are doing can still be wrong. Our motive alone does not determine if we are pleasing God. Saul wanted to know who the Lord was, before he committed his life to Him.

Some skeptics today don't believe that Jesus really existed, but these are the type of skeptics that don't follow history. All serious historians and Bible critics acknowledge that Jesus was crucified on a cross in Jerusalem. Even though some of these historians reject the idea that Jesus is the son of God, they do not deny his existence in history. So who is Jesus? We are told time and again that Jesus is the creator of all the world. We are told in Isaiah 43:11; Isaiah 44:6-8 that there is no other God apart from Yahweh, there was none before Him and there will be none after Him. He calls Himself the first and the last.

However, when we read John 1:1-4, we recognize that Jesus existed with the Father before the world was. Jesus created all things, and nothing was created without Him. He is referred to as the Word that became a human being and lived among them. In John 1:18 it says that He came to reveal the Father to us or to show us what the Father is like. He came in human form so that He could pay the price for our sins and bring us back to God (Philippians 2:5-11).

God the Father called Jesus God and Lord and commanded angels to worship Him (Hebrews 1:6-10). Remember that God alone deserves worship because He does not share His glory with another (Isaiah 42:8). Jesus shares the glory of the Father, the glory He had with Him before the world existed (John 17:5). God the Father sent his Son into the world to rescue people from the penalty of sin. He is the great God and the only Saviour we will ever need

## Additional Questions to Ponder/Discuss

a. What is your relationship with Jesus Christ?
b. Why is it not good to see Jesus only as a good man?
c. Does the Scripture present God as a plural unity?
d. Would you be able to defend the deity of Jesus?
e. Why is it a contradiction if Jesus is the Son and the Father and the Holy Spirit?

# 6.

# What must I do to be saved? —Acts 16:30

## Only One Way

The book of Acts tells us a very intriguing story of a slave girl who was possessed by a demon. She was used by her masters to gain wealth through witchcraft or fortune telling. In chapter 16:18 the Apostle Paul said to the evil spirit,

> "I command you in the name of Jesus Christ to come out of her." And it came out that very hour. When her masters saw that their hope of gain was gone, they dragged Paul and Silas before the rulers and magistrates who then put them into prison. While they were in prison there was a great earthquake that caused all the prisoners' chains or

> locks to break. On seeing the doors open, the guard was about to kill himself, but Paul stopped him. The guard then said "Sirs, what must I do to be saved?" They said, "Believe on the Lord Jesus Christ and you shall be saved, you and your household" (Acts 16:30-32).

They then preach the word of the Lord to the guard and his family and they all believed and were saved.

Many people think that if they behave as good as possible, they will be saved. Some even join a local assembly and become members with the hope that they will receive eternal life. Many have been working in some churches for years with the Hope of securing a place for themselves in heaven.

The question asked in this passage, "What must I do to be saved?" (Acts 16:30) is answered over and over again in Scripture. It was a jailor in Philippi who asked the apostle Paul who was imprisoned what he needed to do to be saved. Then Paul told him to believe in the Lord Jesus, and he will be saved (Acts 16:31). Notice that the man was told to believe and be saved not to **behave** and be saved. We cannot do any amount of good work to be saved. We are saved by the mercy of God and not by our good works. "For by grace you have been saved through faith. And this is not your own doing; it is the gift of God, not a result of works, so that no one may boast (Ephesians 2:8-9). We are saved by grace through faith. This text is simply pointing to the fact that we are not saved by our own works. This is important to note because some people use this verse to teach that God's grace is only offered to some people.

It is abundantly clear in Scripture that it is not God's will that any should perish but that all may come to repentance (1 Peter 3:9). Some invent a teaching that God has two different wills in order to deny the truth that God wants all to repent, but some won't. They ignore verses like John 1:11-12 which state that Jesus came to His own people and they rejected Him, but as many as received Him, He gave the right to become the sons of God. Paul in Romans 10:9-10 says, "If you confess with your mouth that Jesus is Lord and believe in your heart that God has raised him from the dead, you will be saved. For with the heart one believes and is justified, and with the mouth one confesses and is saved."

In Galatians 3:26 the Apostle Paul states clearly that we are children of God by faith. Paul goes on to explain why no one can boast because we have been saved by grace through faith. What this means is that faith or trust in God is a prerequisite to be saved. For it is by faith or trust in Christ that we have access to His grace in which we stand (Romans 5:2). So, we are justified or made right with God through faith and are able to enjoy peace with God (Romans 5:1).

It is extremely important to note that I'm not saying that our faith saves us. It is Jesus who saves us when we put our faith in Him. Nor is it true that Jesus saves us in order that we place our faith in Him. We trust in Jesus first and that is why He saves us. For example, everyone reading this book has placed their trust in something or someone before. When we step on a bridge it is not our faith that holds us up until we reach the other side. We are held up by the bridge when we place our trust in the bridge in order to get over to the other side. This means that it is not the strength of your faith that takes you across, but the strength of the object in which faith is placed, which is the bridge.

Now, Jesus is our bridge through whom we get to the other side. A strong faith is not what gets you across, but a strong bridge. The strength of our faith is only as strong as the object of our faith. In this case the object of our faith is Jesus. He is the one who holds us and takes us to the other side. There was a great divide between us and God and He has bridged the divide that we could be reconciled to God. This is a great place to shout hallelujah!

## Additional Questions to Ponder/Discuss

a. What does God mean by not wanting anyone to perish, but that all should repent?
b. Why can't someone be good enough to be saved?
c. If salvation is by grace through faith, then what role does our good works play in it?
d. Why is it more important to have the right object of faith, than to have a great amount of faith?
e. Since Jesus is willing to save anyone, why are so many people not saved.

# 7.

# Who Is This King of Glory? Psalm 24:8

## Meet King Jesus

There is a very interesting passage of Scripture in Psalm 24:1 where we read, "The earth is the Lord's and the fullness thereof, the world and those who dwell therein." This Psalm tells us that the world was created and that God is the One who created it. The text gives us some insight into the greatness of the creator.

There are many debates today as to how the universe came into being. There are even some who suggest that it has always been here. It will go beyond my purpose for this passage to treat those arguments in a thorough way. However, it is sufficient to state that most modern scientists today believe that the universe had a beginning. There are literally dozens of reasons why scientists believe that. Now, many of them don't necessarily believe that God is the cause of the universe, because they are not prepared to affirm the idea of a supernatural being who is outside of the universe. Whatever they can't prove by scientific methods they are not prepared to affirm, or so they say, so let us meet them where they are.

Many of them claim that there is evidence of a great explosion that gave rise to the universe. The thing is , if nothing existed before the universe, what caused the explosion? What was there to explode? If there was a big bang, what banged ? If there is evidence of a big bang, I know who the banger is.

I know that it is impossible for us to describe what and who God is in a complete way. However, from what we observe in the world and also in the word of God, we have an idea. For example, we know that God must be timeless, spaceless and immaterial because the universe consists of time, space and matter. If God created the world and the world is made up of time, space and matter then God is outside of those things because they were created, and He was not. Looking at the universe can only tell us of God's amazing power but nothing about his amazing love. For that we need special revelation through His word which tells us of the character and love of God.

The Scriptures tell us that in the beginning God created the heavens and the earth (Genesis 1:1). We are also told that Jesus is the one who created all things (John 1:1-3.) It says that nothing that was created was created without Him. There are many other passages in Scripture that tell us that God created the world (Nehemiah 9:6; Ephesians 9:3; Revelations 4:11; Isaiah 37:16; Colossians 1:16; Psalm 8:3-4; Psalm 100:3; Isaiah 42:5; Acts 17:26-28).

Here is a Psalm of David in which he gives us some very important insight as to the Creator and his creation. David starts out by telling us frankly that the earth belongs to God. I know that there are many who are behaving as if it belongs to them, but it belongs to God. In Psalm 100:3 David tells us that we are created by God. He made it and everything that dwells in it, which includes us. We are told in Psalm 24:1 that he created everything. Therefore, we should be thankful to him and praise his name.

The Psalmist asked a question in Psalms 24:3 which requires careful consideration. "Who shall ascend to the hill of the Lord?" He later answered, "He who has clean hands and a pure heart, who does not lift up his soul to what is false and does not swear deceitfully" (v4). We first need to pause and examine ourselves before we answer. In doing that necessary evaluation, we will realize that none of us can truly say that we have not lifted up our soul to that which is false or meaningless. None of us can say that we have no deceit. Only Jesus is perfect and He is able to ascend because He meets the requirements. I don't want you to be dismayed and feel hopeless, because Jesus gave Himself as an offering for our sins and rose from the dead that those who put their trust in Him will be declared right with God (Romans 4:25).

So, although we have no righteousness of our own to enter God's presence, he gave us His righteousness when we trusted Christ for salvation (Romans 5:1; 2 Corinthians 5:21).

Psalm 24:5 says that this person receives blessing and righteousness from the God of his salvation. In a celebratory mode, the Psalmist commanded that the gates lift up their head. He was personifying the gates, as if the gates themselves were rejoicing to see the King.

The Psalmist repeats for emphasis, his appeal to open the gate to let in the King of glory. But when the question, "Who is this King of Glory?" was asked, then came the answer—"The Lord strong and mighty, the Lord mighty in battle" (Psalm 24:8). The Lord of hosts literally is the Lord of armies. This is a beautiful picture of this conquering King who has come back after winning a war. Everyone is celebrating his victory because he is glorious. In Matthew 21:8-10 it says that one day Jesus rode into Jerusalem on a donkey and some people laid down their clothes on the ground while others waved palm branches saying "Hosanna to the Son of David! Blessed is he who comes in the name of the Lord! Hosanna in the highest!" While some people were praising Him others were saying "Who is this?" Some in the crowd acknowledged Jesus as a prophet but they did not understand that He is the King of glory.

If you bow to the King willingly now, you will not have to do it by force in the end. Philippians 2:10 says, " So that at the name of Jesus every knee should bow, in heaven and on earth and under the earth." Those who do not honor Jesus do not honor the Father either. But those who honor the Son honors the Father also (John 5:22-23). Even though Jesus is the Lord of hosts, the God of armies, He did not come to earth to wage war against mankind. When the soldiers came and arrested Him in the garden, He told them that He could have called His heavenly army to fight for Him, but He did not (Matthew 26:53). This shows how strong is His love. It also teaches us that we too must remain focused on God's agenda. He was indeed fighting, but it was not against flesh and blood. He was battling for the souls of mankind. That is why He went all the way to Calvary for you and for me. In the end, we see the king being worshipped. So let us join the celebration and welcome Jesus the king, in our lives.

## Additional Questions to Ponder/Discuss

a. Why do people need to let in the King of Glory?
b. How can we be made fit for the glorious presence of God?
c. Do you believe that the universe always existed? Why or why not?
d. Can something come into existence without a cause?
e. Why did Jesus come to earth in human flesh?

# 8.

# Where do you get that living water? —John 4:11

## The Source of Life

Probably more bad things have been spoken about the Samaritan woman than all other women in the New Testament. Many of which by the way are not found in the pages of Scripture. For example, we have heard it preached that this woman goes about the community stealing other women's husbands. This they say because the text said that she has had five husbands. We have also heard that she came to the well at that time of the day because she wanted to avoid being seen by people in the community who would scorn her. We are also told by some that the man she is now living with was someone else's husband. I know that this woman was not living a very upright life but could we just stop piling bad things onto her reputation since it is already smeared.

Let us look at what the text actually said. In John 4:16-18 tells us that Jesus says to her "Go call your husband, and come here." The woman answered him, "I have no husband". Jesus said to her, "You are right in saying, I have no husband; for you have had five husbands, and the one you now have is not your husband. What you have said is true."

It said that she had five husbands which simply means that she was married five times. It is possible that all these men used her and then left her. We don't know if she was disgraceful or disloyal in those relationships. Secondly, suggesting that her questionable character was the reason for the time of day that she came to the well is just pure speculation. She may have come to the well at that time on that day for a particular reason, we just don't know. We must not seek to second guess her motive. The man who is presently living with her was not married to her. This does not mean that he was married to someone else.

In verses 11 and 12 the lady asked Jesus "Sir, you have nothing to draw with, and the well is deep. Where do you get that living water? Are you greater than our father Jacob? Let us look at a couple of important questions that she asked Jesus. Firstly, she asked "From where are you going to get this water?" She followed up with a second question because she was not aware of the truth concerning the first question. Her second question, "Are you greater than our father Jacob?" shows she didn't know that Jesus is the source of living water. He offers water that does not come from a pot or pond or well. He is the well that never runs dry.

## Additional Questions to Ponder/Discuss

a. Do you sometimes scoff at this Samaritan woman? Why?
b. Why did Jesus ask her to go and call her husband?
c. Is there a difference between worshipping on the mountain and worshipping on the plain?
d. Why does God only seek worshippers that worship in spirit and in truth?
e. What does Jesus mean when he said his food is to do the will of the Father?

# 9.

# What must I do with Jesus? —Matthew 27:21-22

## The choice that decides our destiny

What must I do with Jesus? This is a very important and crucial question that everyone urgently needs to answer. It is a question for the saved and for the unsaved, because everyone will give an account for what he or she does with Jesus. This is a question we are confronted with in Matthew 27:21-22 The governor asked the people "Which of the two do you want me to release for you? And they said, Barabbas." Pilate said to them, "Then what must I do with Jesus who is called the Christ?" They said "let Him be crucified".

The text before us tells us that Jesus stood before Pilate as he asked the crowd what he should do with Jesus. The question was asked after he did his own investigation and recognized that Jesus was only brought before him because the Jews were jealous of the work Jesus was doing among the people (Matthew 27:18).

After Pilate assessed the situation, he realized that Jesus was innocent of the charges against Him so Pilate told the crowd that he found no fault in Him (Luke 23: 4). Pilate admired Jesus but he still appeased the Jews because he gave Jesus over to them to be crucified. He gave Jesus to them because he was more concerned with being a friend of Caesar than being a friend of God. The Jews threatened to tell Caesar if he let Jesus go free (John 19:12). Pilate wanted to do the right thing, but he did the wrong thing because of his own agenda. He was a man pleaser and not a God pleaser.

Just thinking about doing good isn't good enough if we are not pleasing God. This is seen in the text because Pilate referred to Jesus as a just man. In Matthew 27:19 Pilate said he found no fault in Jesus. His wife called Jesus a just man (Matt 27:19). Judas said that Jesus was innocent (Matthew 27:4). Nevertheless, they all refuse to follow their conviction to make the right decision.

Many people will be separated from God through all eternity even though they think that Jesus is good and Jesus is God. Thinking that Jesus is good is not enough unless it leads to trust in Jesus. There is someone in the story who responded the right way to Jesus on that day. The thief on the right of Jesus, who was also hanging on a cross, chose to believe in Jesus and trusted Him for salvation. This goes to show that even if you have a bad attitude towards Jesus, He is willing and ready to forgive you if you put your trust in Him and turn from sin.

We must be careful when we ask the question what to do with Jesus. When we want to make a life decision, be careful not to ask the wrong crowd and therefore get a wrong answer. The crowd told Pilate to crucify Jesus. We are all committed to either please the crowd, ourselves or God. Therefore, don't ask those who are sneering at Jesus, ask those who are surrendered to Him. Don't ask the people who are laughing at Jesus, ask the ones that are listening to him. Don't ask those who reject Jesus, ask those who receive Him.

So, if you ask me what you must do with Jesus, I am happy to tell you that you should trust him for salvation and surrender yourself to Him to be used by Him for the glory of God. In light of what He has done for you by protecting and preserving and providing for you, it is only reasonable to serve Him (Romans 12:1-2). While we were still sinners Christ died for us (Romans 5:8). This means that He was thinking about us even when we were not thinking about Him. This was Jesus' commitment because we can only be saved by His grace alone through faith (Ephesians 2:8-9). Salvation is found in Jesus alone for there is no other name given among men under heaven whereby we must be saved (Acts 4:12). Jesus is the only way to the Father and no one can come to the Father apart from coming through Jesus (John 14: 6). So, in light of this truth, what will you do with Jesus?

## Additional Questions to Ponder/Discuss

a. What have you done with Jesus?
b. Why is choosing Jesus so urgent and important?
c. Why did Pilate seek to please the crowd?
d. Should Pilate be considered righteous, since he confessed that Jesus was a just man?
e. Was Pilate innocent of the blood of Jesus?

# 10. How can someone feed these people in a desolate place? —Mark 8:4

## The Bread of Life

One day Jesus was preaching and there was a large crowd listening to Him and it got late. Neither the disciples nor the people had sufficient food to feed the crowd. The disciples wanted to send the crowd away. Then the disciples asked, "How can one feed these people with bread here in a desolate place?" Jesus rebuked them for their lack of trust, for their lack of perception and for constantly forgetting what God has done in the past for them.

This question was asked after they had already witnessed the feeding of several thousands of people with only five loaves and two fish. This experience in the desert points out one of the failings of the disciples.

It is important to point out that the word that is used for men in Mark 8:4 actually refers to males. Therefore, given the fact that these situations usually have women and children also, it could be many more than just 5,000 who were fed that day.

So here they are again in a similar situation where a large crowd was gathered and was with Jesus for three days. It is evident that this crowd was there to listen and learn from Jesus because for the three days they were with Him and they had no food (v1). Jesus told His disciples that He had compassion on them. That means that He could feel their pain, feel their hunger. Now I wonder why Jesus saw it fit to tell His disciples how He felt about the people and their situation. Could it be because He wanted the disciples to have the same care for the people as He did?

As people of God, we need to follow our Saviour. We should love what He loves and care for what He cares about, and He surely does love and care about people. So while the disciples wanted Jesus to send the people away, Jesus was saying, "If I send them away hungry they will faint."(v3) To understand what was going on in this situation, we must see what the disciples are saying. The disciples were saying, "We don't have enough." They were saying, "Jesus is not enough." Although they had witnessed the power and authority of Jesus in the past, they still thought that was not enough. Isn't it sad that in spite of the evidence of Christ's love and power displayed in our circumstances we still think that He is not enough?

At this point I want to turn your attention to a passage of Scripture in 2 Kings 4:42-44. In this test, Elisha had a crisis on his hands. There were 100 soldiers and not enough bread. Does this start to sound familiar yet? It gets better. The servant asked Elisha, "Should I set this before 100 men?" He had asked this question because he thought the bread was not enough. But Elisha repeated that they should serve the bread to the people. The bread shared for all the soldiers and they had leftovers.

It is amazing what God can do when we give to Him the little we have and honestly trust Him to use it. He will use our little gifts and talents. The greatness is not seen in the amount we have to offer, it is seen in how we offer, and to whom we offer it. Notice that Jesus gave thanks for the little he had, so He came with gratitude. That was His attitude, and He gave it to his Father. We must do the same if we want God to do amazing things in our life. Remember that the little we have can do much if we give it to God.

There is so much beauty in seeing manifestations of Old Testament teachings and types in the New Testament. For example, God gave the Israelites bread in the wilderness when they had no food. God provided manna which was really bread supernaturally provided for them in the wilderness journey. Jesus also provided food for thousands of people in a desolate place. When God sent down bread from heaven, the people responded by saying "what is it?"(Exodus 16:15). In the New Testament, we read in John's gospel where Jesus told us that He is the bread of life that came down from heaven. He also says that whosoever receives this bread will never die (John 6:48-51). By this He means will not die spiritually or be separated from Him.

Many places around the world today Jesus is treated in the same way the Israelites in the wilderness treated manna with Scorn or contempt. If we put our trust in Jesus, we shall have eternal life and not come into judgment. The fact is that Jesus is the true Bread of Heaven and apart from Him we cannot have eternal life. Is He enough? Can you offer this "Bread" to people who have hungry souls and are dying in this desolate place? Yes, you can and you should. Jesus is saying to us, don't send them away hungry; offer them this Bread.

## Additional Questions to Ponder/Ask

a. When do you find it most difficult to trust God?
b. What does it mean that Jesus is the Bread of life?
c. Can you have great faith and still not get what you want?
d. How has God shown himself to be your provider in difficult circumstances?
e. What will you offer for God to use today?

# PART 3:
# DEALING WITH WORRY AND FEAR

# 11.
# Do you not care that we are perishing? —Mark 4:38

## Trusting God in Troublesome Times

One day Jesus told His disciples that they were going over to the other side of the lake. While on the journey, a storm came and the boat was filling up with water. They became very fearful and woke Jesus who was sleeping in the stern of the boat. They said to him "Teacher, do you not care that we are perishing? (Mark 4:38). Can you feel the intense emotion in that question, the anxiety and fear that causes him to question God's goodness to him?

One day I was in my living room and I heard a desperate cry for help. It was my six-year-old daughter in deep distress. I ran to her room and saw her gasping for breath while holding up the seven-drawer chest of draws that was falling over on her. I came to her rescue and lifted the weight off her. She was so happy that day to know that I was near and that I could hear her cry. Maybe if we stopped to think for a while, we might remember that in our own life circumstances, we have asked if God is really here and does He even care.

The problem with this type of thinking though, is that it assumes that God does not have our best interest at heart. These thoughts will dominate our mind when we forget God's goodness towards us in the past. These disciples would have already experienced Christ's provision and protection which should have given enough evidence that Jesus cares. One might ask the question, "Does Jesus really care?" I can answer for myself that He does.

This is why Paul implores us in Philippians 4:6, "Do not be anxious about anything, but in everything by prayer and supplication with thanksgiving let your request be made known to God. The result of that approach to anxiety gives us a picture of peace being personified as guards watching and protecting something that is precious, which is your heart and mind." It says "And the peace of God, which surpasses all understanding will guard your hearts and minds in Christ Jesus." When we are in difficult times, we want to have not just the God of peace on our journey, but the peace of God that protects our hearts and minds in Jesus Christ.

Jesus had a plan for this particular journey with His disciples and He also has a plan for our life journey as well.

Let us look at some of the lessons that can help us in our difficult situations today. First thing to note is that it was Jesus who told them that they were going over to the other side. They then went on the journey with Jesus and a storm came. This goes to show that we can be in the will of God traveling with Jesus and storms come into our lives. This implies that storms in your life are not an indicator of your obedience or disobedience to God. The storms of life come to everyone.

There is something we need to remember when we face a storm: remember what He has said to us. He told them that they were going over to the other side, therefore it did not matter how much the storm beat against them or how much the boat was rocking, they were going to make it over. The text tells us that the boat was now full (Mark 4:37). Have you ever felt like that, when it's as if you just could not take any more? Then you can identify with these disciples. Beware lest you forget that the Lord has promised that He will never leave us nor forsake us (Hebrews 13:5-6.) He can sympathize with us because He knows how it feels, (Hebrews 4:15.) We need to rest our security in Him, for unless the Lord keeps us, we cannot be kept. The Psalmist makes the point that unless the Lord watches the city, the watchman stays awake in vain (Psalm 127:1).

While king David was being persecuted by Saul, he was in near-death situations often but he said, "When I am afraid, I put my trust in God" (Psalm 56:3.) We must not allow fear to captivate our minds. We are told in Isaiah 26:3 that God will comfort us. It says "You keep him in perfect peace whose mind is stayed on you, because he trusts in you." I remember when I was held up at gunpoint twice; I did not know if I would make it out alive, but God delivered me. I remember there was a time when I was so worried about various things in my life that I did not have control over. I was worried about my children; if they will be okay when I'm gone, but God comforted me. He assured me that He cares about them more than I do.

I wish to leave you with a verse I hold dear to my heart because it has helped me in my troubled times. Psalm 4:8 says, "In peace I will both lie down and sleep; for you alone, O Lord, make me dwell in safety." So, the next time you begin to wonder if Jesus cares you can answer with confidence and say, "oh yes He cares."

## Additional Questions to Ponder/Discuss

a. Do you sometimes feel like God does not care about you?
b. What do you do when you are anxious?
c. How do you feel when you obey God and storms still come into your life?
d. Does the Bible teach that if we obey God, we will not have trouble?
e. What did Jesus want to teach them on the journey?

# 12. Which of you can add an hour to your lifespan by worrying? —Matthew 6:27

## The Waste of Worrying

Worrying comes so easy for some people and for others it is so comforting that they have something to worry about. If everything is going on fine, they will begin to worry that they have nothing to worry about. In Matthew 6:25-34 Jesus gave a word of comfort to those who are worried and anxious about the everyday concerns of life. In verses 25-26 it says

> "Therefore I tell you, do not be anxious about your life, what you will eat or what you will drink, nor about your body what you will put on. Is not life more than clothing? Look at the birds of the air: they neither

> sow nor reap nor gather into barns, and yet your heavenly Father feeds them. Are you not of more value than they?"

The text before us is a well-known passage of Scrip-ture but it is often misunderstood.

Jesus dealt with some very practical things about the issue of worrying that we can personally identify with. He pointed out some things that people often worry about. Let us look at that list. The first thing Jesus mentions is worrying about life in general. We fear death and so we often worry about losing our lives. The devil has used this fear often to hold people in captivity to sin (Hebrews 2:15). Jesus asked, "Which of you by worrying can add a single hour to his span of life?" (Matthew 6:27) The second thing people worry about is food. Food is important to survive but worrying about what you will eat, or drink shows a lack of trust in God. The third thing on the list is worry about clothing. Even those who have clothes often worry about which of the clothes they should wear on a particular occasion. Some people don't have enough clothes and they worry, while others have too much, and they worry as well. Jesus pointed their attention to observe the birds and flowers and see how God cares for things that are of less importance than people (v 28:30).

People can apply what Jesus has said here and experience the peace and provision of God even in difficult situations. Jesus wants us to let Him be our Shelter, our Rock, our Fortress, our Source of help in times of trouble. When we are lonely, when we are sick, when we need a job and when we feel hopeless, He says to us that our security must be in Him and not in the things we possess.

He says in Matthew 6:19-20, "Do not lay up for yourself treasures on earth, where moth and rust destroy and where thieves break in and steal, but lay up for yourself treasures in heaven where neither moth nor rust destroy and where thieves do not break in and steal." If we are going to do this, we must seek first the kingdom of God and his righteousness (v 33). It is about setting our affections on the things above, that is, on God's agenda and not on our own desires (Colossians 3:1-2). When we seek God's agenda then He gives to us the things we need (Matthew 6:33). Our heart will follow what and who we treasure, (v 21). So, let's treasure the Lord and His agenda.

We are also told to respond to worry by giving it to the Lord. I Peter 5:7 says "Casting all anxiety on him, because he cares for you." When we cast our burdens on the Lord, He will sustain us (Psalm 55:22). Paul implored the believers to not worry about anything but to pray about everything. He gives us the answer to our worry. He says that when we trust God and bring everything to God, the peace of God will guard our hearts and minds in Christ Jesus (Philippians 4:6-7). So why do you worry? Can you make your situation better by worrying? Worrying often brings sickness, depression and pain, so take your burdens to the Lord.

## Additional Questions to Ponder/Discuss

a. Do you feel better when you worry?
b. What are the things that worry you most?
c. What does Peter say about worry in 1 Peter 5:7?
d. How can we have peace in the midst of our problem?
e. Are you comforted by the fact that God takes care of even the birds and the flowers?

# PART 4:

# DEALING WITH GRATITUDE AND GREED

# 13. What do you want me to do for you? —Luke 18:41

## The Invitation to Ask

In this story in Luke 18 we meet a blind beggar. One day as he sat by the roadside, he heard a great crowd passing by. When he heard the noise, he asked what was going on and they told him that Jesus was passing by. He then called to Jesus for help, but the crowd told him to shut up. But the blind man really had a desire to meet Jesus. He had heard about Jesus and therefore wanted to meet Him because he knew Jesus could help Him. However, the crowd was a hindrance to his goal.

Having made a decision to call out to Jesus, he had to have a bit of determination because the crowd wanted him to shut up. When you are in a situation where you have a desire to seek after Jesus, you have to make a decision to put that desire to action and be determined not to allow anyone or anything to stop you. You might have noticed that the people who were hindering him from going to Christ were people who were around Jesus. People who were walking with him. This goes to show that not everyone that is around Christ understands what His goal is for people. The crowd was not speaking for Jesus even though they might have thought so.

The man cried out even louder and his determination caught Jesus's attention. It is important to note that while others were saying no to the blind man, Jesus was saying yes. While they were saying stay where you are, in the same state and situation, Jesus said come to me. While the crowd was telling the man to shut up, Jesus told him to speak up. Therefore, Jesus asked him "What do you want me to do for you?" (Luke 18:41)

At this point he had an option and an opportunity to tell Jesus exactly what he wanted. Since the man was begging on the roadside, he could have requested to be blessed with enough money that he will not have any more financial need. However, the man requested one thing—he said, "Lord I want to see." Isn't that a wonderful request? When he received his sight, the text said that he followed Jesus. Note that when he was delivered, he followed Jesus and not the crowd. The crowd praised God when they saw what Jesus did in his life. So, what do you want Jesus to do for you?

## Additional Questions to Ponder/Ask

a. Why did Jesus stop for the blind man?
b. Is it possible to be around Jesus, and not know what pleases him?
c. Do you allow what people say to stop you from coming to Jesus?
d. What are the obstacles that are preventing you from coming to Jesus?
e. Why should we seek God's desire for our lives instead of our own desires?

# 14.
# The things you have prepared, whose will they be? —Luke 12:13-21

## Bank with God

It is a good thing to have money, but it becomes dangerous when money has us. Jesus told this story because He wanted to warn the crowd not to be covetous because it has devastating consequences. Covetousness has led people into bitterness, hatred, malice and murder. We are warned to guard ourselves from covetousness and jealousy. There is a portion of Scripture in the book of Philippians which helps us to guard ourselves (Philippians 4:5-8). It says that we should rejoice at all times, that is, seek to be glad about who you are and what you have. It means to celebrate God regardless of our circumstances.

Jesus went a bit deeper when dealing with the problem of greed as he made the point that we must not run after material things (v 15). The man in the story was very rich and that was all that he lived for. Nothing is wrong with having money, the problem is when money starts having you, when it controls your mind and dictates your decisions. The man sought to expand the place he stored his wealth. So, picture someone today whose only focus is expanding and increasing his bank accounts to store more of his wealth. Many people today live their life like the man in this story.

I want us to notice a sad reality that the man did not realize. He did not see that all the wealth he was storing up on earth, he will someday die and leave it. People need to understand that they can't take their earthly possessions with them when they die. Even if someone places money or jewels inside the dead person's coffin, that person cannot use the money or wear the jewels in the grave.

A careful observation of the text reveals something else. That is, he told himself a lie. He deceived himself into thinking that money could solve all his problems. He also fooled himself into thinking that he had more time than he really did. For he was saying to himself, "Soul you have ample goods laid up for many years; relax, eat, drink and be merry." But God said to him, "Fool! This night your soul is required of you, and the things you have prepared, whose will they be?" (Luke 12:19-20).

It is important to note that the word that is translated fool in this verse does not mean stupid, it means crazy. So what Jesus is saying is that when someone lives his or her life for just earthly riches but is poor towards God, that person is crazy (v 21). In Mark 8:36-37 we read, "For what shall it profit a man to gain the whole world and lose his own soul? Or what can a man give in exchange for his soul?" (Mark 8:36-37, KJV). A person's soul is worth more than all the wealth he can possess on this earth. This is why Jesus wants us to bank with him in heaven and not just on earth (v 21). It is true that sometimes even Christians get discouraged when they are poor in earthly wealth, even if they are rich towards God, but in the end, it will be devastating to those people, who only possess earthly riches but are poor towards God (v 21).

Here is a sober warning from the Apostle Paul. He said that those who run after or crave riches on earth fall into temptation, into traps and many senseless and harmful desires that plunge people into ruin and destruction. Through the crave of money, some have wandered away from the faith and have hurt themselves severely, (1 Timothy 6:6-10). Godliness with contentment is great gain. Therefore, let us seek God, love people and use money well.

## Additional Questions to Ponder/Discuss

a. What is your view on Christians being very rich?
b. What is your view on Christians being poor?
c. What does 1 Timothy 6:9-10 say about people who strive to be rich?
d. Do you have an insatiable desire to be rich?

e. Are you storing your treasures in heaven by living for God?

# PART 5:
# DEALING WITH SURRENDER AND SERVICE

# 15.

# Are you still sleeping?

## Mark 14:41

## Assessment on the Job

It was nearing the time of Jesus' crucifixion. This was a crucial time in the lives of Jesus and His disciples. He had earlier told His disciples that He was going to be crucified and then rise again. But the disciples didn't want to hear that, so they resisted what Jesus was saying. Peter also rebuked Jesus for talking about His death (Mark 8:31-33). The Scriptures tell us that all have sinned and come short of the glory of God (Romans 3:23), and the wages of sin is death (Romans 6:23). The only way to save sinners was to pay for their sin debt. So, Jesus chose to bear the penalty so that we can have salvation through faith in him.

Jesus then went to share His last Passover with his disciples, at which time He also instituted the Lord's Supper which is what we refer to as communion today (Mark 14:22-

25). As they finished supper they went to the Mount of Olives. It was at this time that he predicted that Peter would deny him. He did this because Peter was being proud and self-dependent. Jesus tried to bring him to his senses so that he would humble himself, but Peter refused to listen. In Mark 14:27 we read that Jesus said to them, "You will all fall away, for it is written, I will smite the shepherd and the sheep will be scattered." Peter said to him, "Even though they all fall away, I will not" (v29).

While they were in the garden the emotional pressure of the crucifixion came crashing down on Jesus, so he asked his disciples Peter, James and John to join Him (Mark 14:32-34). These men were so privileged to be called out from the rest of the disciples to watch with Jesus. Can you imagine being called aside by Jesus to spend time with him, to have fellowship with Him? There could be no greater joy. An important piece of information to note here, is that Jesus had already told them what was coming (Matthew 26:31-46). He also told Peter that the devil wants to sift him as wheat (Luke 22:31). He warned them in the garden to watch and pray so that they don't come into temptation and fall or fail (Mark 14:38).

So what does Jesus mean by watch? Well, it doesn't just mean look. He means be vigilant, be alert, and be aware. This is what we also read in 1 Peter 5:8, "Be sober-minded; be watchful. Your adversary the devil prowls around like a roaring lion, seeking someone to devour." We need to be alert at all times because we are not ignorant of the devil's schemes (2 Corinthians 2:11). Jesus was telling them to stay on guard. But notice where they are at that time, they are in the presence of Jesus (Mark 14:38). There are some Christians who believe that the devil is just waiting for them to leave the church to attack them. If you are inside the church building and thinking like that, the devil has already attacked and deceived you. The enemy will fight us wherever we are: home, church, school, on the mission field or on the playfield. This is why we need to put on the whole armor of God so that we are able to take a stand for God and to withstand the devil (Ephesians 6:10-18).

Jesus told them why they need to be vigilant. He also informed them that the flesh is weak. We cannot wrestle against the enemy in our own strength, but it gets even worse. When we are physically weak, we are more likely to not be alert spiritually. Please don't get me wrong, I am not saying that if we are weak physically, then we are also weak spiritually; far from it. What I am saying, and maybe you will also agree, that when we are fatigued and feel drained and burnt-out, we can fall into temptation more easily. When a person has had a long hard and stressful day, that makes him more likely to have less patience with the other drivers on the road, who are trying to bully him off the road. The good news is that although the flesh is weak, the spirit is willing; willing to watch, willing to war for God, willing to wait on God. This means that we can do it. Oh yes we can!

This story tells us four things through which we can have victory in Jesus. Firstly, we can have victory through surrender to God. Notice that at no point was Peter surrendered to God. He ignored the warning that Satan wants to sift him as wheat (Luke 22:31). He rebuked Jesus for prophesying about his coming crucifixion (Matthew 16:20-23). Peter also insisted that he knew himself better than Jesus knew him, for when Jesus told Peter that he was going to desert Him like the rest of the disciples would, Peter disagreed (Mark 14:29). Can you imagine saying to Jesus, "You don't know me like I know me?"

Secondly, we can have victory through suffering. Jesus demonstrated this to us. He was reviled, insulted, despised, lied on, opposed, spat upon and humiliated. However, he triumphed through sacrifice and suffering. When He was in the garden, He was crying out in pain before a whip was laid on his back. But he said, "Father not my will, but thine be done." Hallelujah! Praise God! He counted the cost. He became our substitute and bore the wrath of God that was poured out against sin, not on sinners. It was the Savior who paid it all. Jesus paid the price in full and we owe everything to Him

Thirdly, we can have victory through obedience to God. We are exhorted by the Apostle Peter to regard Christ in our heart as holy (1 Peter 3:15). Peter was not treating Jesus as Lord of his life; he was just responding to Jesus as his pal. Jesus is more than just our friend. When we resist Jesus' agenda, we miss the meaning of Jesus being Lord of our life. For if he is indeed Lord, then we must not tell him no; no and Lord don't go well in this context. If we are going to live an obedient lifestyle, we must be yielded to God.

Fourthly, we can have victory through service to God. Notice again how Jesus demonstrated this. He chose to serve even in the most unpleasant circumstances. This he was able to do because the service pleased the Father. Peter, James and John on the other hand failed this lesson. They were sleeping on the job (Mark 14:37-41). I wrote a song some years ago in which the chorus says, "I've been sleeping when I should be working, I've been cruising when I should be reaching the lost and I've been hiding when I should be fighting, I've been gazing away all my time."

Look at what happened when the soldiers came for Jesus. Peter chopped off one of the soldier's ears. But Jesus rebuked him and told him to put up his sword (John 18:10-11). Peter may have thought that what he did was pleasing to Jesus, but it wasn't. Maybe even the rest of the disciples were impressed with Peter's actions, but Jesus was not. All we need to do each day is to make Jesus smile; to please him by what we do, think and say.

If what we do does not make Jesus smile, it doesn't matter who else smiles. If He is not pleased, it doesn't matter who else is. How did Peter get here? It started by refusing to surrender to Christ completely. If we fail in our surrender, we will experience spiritual failure in every other area of our life. Since his life was not surrendered to Christ, his service was not pleasing to Christ. This is why Peter was using the wrong weapon. He took out the wrong sword because he was not engaged in the right fight. For we do not wrestle against flesh and blood (Ephesians 6:12). Finally, I want to share something that can help us to be victorious. We are sure that Jesus was able to run a good race because his eyes were fixed on the finish line. He ran well because of where he was looking. He was looking at the prize and the joy that was set before him (Hebrews 12:3).

I remember being at a sports day with a friend to watch his son run. When the race started his son was at the front of the pack, on his way to win. But he got distracted by all the people who were shouting and cheering for him. So, while he was busy running and looking and listening to the cheering of the crowd, he lost the race. His father went to him, but he did not scold him because the child was only six years old. He said to his son, "I am going to be at the finish line waiting for you, so when the starter says go you must just keep looking at the finish line and just keep running." I guess you know how his next race ended. He won, not because he was running faster than before, but he was now running more focused than before.

You see, we too are in this race and we need to run with our eyes fixed on Jesus, the author and finisher of our faith. Jesus is also waiting for us at the finish line. So "let us also lay aside every weight, and sin which clings so closely, and let us run with endurance the race that is set before us" (Hebrews 12:1-2). For there are many who have gone before us and they are cheering us on in glory. So, the question is; are you still sleeping?

## Additional Questions to Ponder/Discuss

a. Was Jesus unreasonable to ask the disciples to stay alert?

b. In what area in your life do you have a struggle to resist the Devil?
c. Have you surrendered that area to God?
d. If we are tired physically, how can we still fight spiritually?
e. Can we live victoriously even if we don't submit to God?

# 16.
# Whom shall I send, and who will go for us? —Isaiah 6:8

## When we say yes to God

The year king Uzziah died Isaiah saw the Lord, the King of glory, the Lord of host. Isaiah was witnessing a worship Tscene of the Lord on His throne (Isa 61:1-4). In theology what Isaiah saw is called a theophany. It is a physical manifestation of the Saviour before the incarnation at Bethlehem. Jesus tells us in John 1:18, "No one has ever seen God; the only God, who is at the Father's side, he has made him known." Therefore, all the manifestations of God in the Old Testament were actually theophanies of Jesus Christ. In fact, we are told in the New Testament that on this occasion Isaiah saw Jesus (John 12:41).

Isaiah became terrified and thought that he would die because he was a sinful man in the presence of a holy and awesome God. When Isaiah saw the Lord for who He is, he also saw himself for who he is (v5). Isaiah was not destroyed but rather cleansed of his sins. This is a picture that shows why sinful man could not just be brought in the presence of the holy God in heaven. A person who does not have his sins forgiven through trusting in the atoning work of Jesus Christ cannot stand in the courts of God. This would be torture instead of joy and bliss, because he has no covering and no righteousness imputed to him to make him fit for the dwelling place of God.

After Isaiah was cleansed, he heard the Lord ask the question, "Whom shall I send, and who will go for us?" (v8). Notice that God was asking for someone to volunteer for the mission. He wants to send people who are willing to go. We can get involved in a mission for God in our homeland, in our own community and workplace and in our home or school. We don't have to cross the sea to share the gospel. We only need to see the cross to share the gospel.

So, who should go? You should go. I should go. Those who have been cleansed should go, because we have met the Lord of glory. When should we go and tell? If you have been washed by the blood of Jesus, then you should have been going already. Where should we go and tell? It is as we live our lives, we share the gospel. It is wherever we find ourselves.

This is not a responsibility that we should carry out only in the local assembly. We are to share the gospel with our lips and our lives. Why should we go and tell? Like Isaiah, we are grateful and thankful that the Lord has forgiven us. We also recognize that it is a miserable and dreadful situation for someone to come in the presence of a holy God unclothed without the righteousness of Jesus Christ. So, since we understand this, we seek to persuade people to trust in Jesus (2 Corinthians 5:11). Not only do we share the message because we are grateful for our salvation, and fearful that others will be lost, but we are commanded by Jesus to make disciples (Matthew 28: 18-20).

Now, we can only make disciples if we first make converts, and we cannot make converts if they don't hear the gospel, and how will they hear the gospel if we don't preach it? (Romans 10:14). The Scripture tells us in Romans 1:16 that the gospel is the power of God for salvation to everyone who believes.

Finally, we seek to win people to Christ because we are told that those who win people to Christ are wise, and those who turn many to righteousness shall shine like the stars forever (Daniel 12:3). As we go, what must we tell them? Tell them about the plight they are in, that all have sinned and come short of the glory of God (Romans 3:23). That the wages of sin, is death (Romans 6:23). That it is appointed unto man to die once and after that is judgement (Hebrews 9:27).

Tell them that God has made a provision for human beings to be forgiven of their sins and spend eternity with Him (John 3:15-17; Romans 5:8). John 3:16 says, "For God so loved the world, that He gave his only son, that whosoever believes in Him should not perish but have eternal life." Tell them that Jesus is the only way to heaven. Jesus himself said, "I am the way the truth and the life, no one comes to the father except through me" (John 14:6). Jesus is the beautiful gate through whom everyone must come because He is the door to heaven (John 10:9). We are told in Acts that there is no other name under heaven given among men whereby we must be saved. This is because there is no salvation apart from Jesus. Salvation is found in nothing and no one else (Acts 4:12).

Here is a word of warning. The thing God rewards is our faithfulness to His will and word. He will not reward us because our ministry was a success in our community. What am I saying here? Notice that God told Isaiah that the people to whom he was sent, will not listen to him (Isaiah 6:9-11). As we read the account of Isaiah's ministry, the people did not obey or listen to him for the most part. But please do not miss this, **God rewards your faithfulness to him, not just your success in ministry.** So, when you hear the Lord ask today, 'Who shall I send and who will go?' will you respond by saying to him, "here am I, I will go?"

## Additional Questions to Ponder/Discuss

a. Have you ever felt terrified in the presence of God?
b. Why is it essential that we share the gospel?
c. Why is it crucial that we be clean as we preach the gospel?

d. Is our success in ministry more important than our faithfulness to God?
e. Are you making disciples for Jesus?

# 17.
# Where are you?
# — Genesis 3:9

## It's Not About Your Location

In Genesis chapter 3 we read the story of the sin of the first couple in scripture. Adam and his wife Eve fell out of intimate fellowship with God when they disobeyed His command. We read in Genesis 2:15 The Lord God took the man and put him in the garden of Eden to work it and keep it. And the Lord God commanded the man, saying, "You may surely eat of every tree of the garden, but of the tree of the knowledge of good and evil you shall not eat, for in the day you eat of it you shall surely die." After they had disobeyed the command of God, they tried to hide from Him. The Lord called out to Adam and said "Where are you?"

Questions are very important and they are used for various reasons. "Where are you?" is the first question we see God ask in Scripture. It was not a question to find out

Adam's geographical or physical location but to help him see his spiritual condition. The question was meant to expose Adam and Eve to themselves. They had disobeyed God and were hiding. It is important to note that God knew where they were since He is omniscient. This response from the first pair has continued even to this day. Not only do we see their response in hiding or running away from God, but they also made excuses and blamed others for their sin. That is a behaviour that is commonly practiced today. People often refuse to take responsibility for their wrong doing.

We are happy that God did not leave them in their state of hiding and nakedness. He sought them and exposed them to their sinful condition, and then provided a covering for their nakedness and made an offering for their sin. Today we don't rely on the blood of animals but on the shed blood of Christ of which the animal sacrifices are a foreshadow. So, as you look at yourself, how would you answer the question, "Where are you?"

God has given to us commands just like he gave Adam and Eve. He has given to us instructions about things that we are not to allow in our lives. Things such as pride, jealousy, envy, hatred, lust, and other things that he forbids us to do. Where are you concerning that instruction? He also commands us to do something for Him. To take care of the fatherless, the widows and those who cannot help themselves (James 1:27). So where are you concerning that? Are you like Adam and Eve no longer enjoying his fellowship because you have moved away from his agenda? Let us seek his forgiveness and return to his agenda. There is a place for resting to rejuvenate one's self, but not to put God's work on pause. Wherever we are and whatever we do, must be done to the glory of God, for there is no vacation from this vocation. We must not take a holiday from doing God's will.

God doesn't just want to see us in church, He wants to see us in His will. God was not satisfied with seeing Adam and Eve in the garden, He wanted to see them in His will. He is not satisfied in seeing us in a good place. He wants us to accomplish His purpose which includes reaching the lost at all cost. This question "where are you?" is relevant for us today, because God wants us to evaluate our spiritual condition. It's not about where we are sitting now, it's about who we are pleasing now. God sometimes asks questions, not because he needs information, but because he wants us to see our condition.

## Additional Questions to Ponder/Discuss

a. Why do people run from God instead of running to him?
b. Why does God want us to know where we are?
c. Does the fact that God sees your every move impact your decisions?
d. In terms of service and obedience to God, where are you?
e. How can we be more effective in service to God?

# 18. How can this be since I am a virgin? — Luke 1:34

## God Has Saved Me Too

The teaching of the miraculous conception of Mary has caused a great deal of misunderstanding and debates for centuries. Some Roman Catholics have elevated Mary to the level of the godhead, making her a mediator through whom the saints can get their prayers to be acceptable to God. But the Bible tells us that there is only one mediator between God and man, and that is Jesus Christ (1Timothy 2:5). Some Roman Catholics also refer to Mary as 'the mother of God' to emphasize her status and worth. We need to understand that God is the creator of the heavens and the earth and all that dwell in it. Since Mary was created, she could not then be the mother of God.

This can be a little technical here and might need some clarification. In John we are told that the Word was in the beginning with God and the Word was God. All things were made by Him and nothing was made without Him (John 1:1-3). In verse 14 it says that the Word became flesh and dwelt among us and we beheld his glory as of the only begotten of the father, full of grace and truth. This was necessary because mankind had sinned against God and needed a Saviour because we are not able to save ourselves. So, we will agree that she is highly favored or graced. She is blessed among women, not above all women. She was privileged to be the vessel through whom the Saviour would come. But she too needed a Saviour, (Luke 1:47).

Therefore, Mary must be honored but she must not be worshipped. The idea of giving Mary the title "Queen of Heaven" is not praiseworthy; it is a pagan idea that comes from idol worshippers (Jerimiah 44:17-19).

There are other issues with seeing Mary as perfect, since the Scriptures tell us that all have sinned and come short of God's glory (Romans 3:23). The only person who has never sinned is Jesus (Hebrews 4:15, 1 Pet. 3:18). On the view that Mary was a perpetual virgin; it is clear that Mary had other children after she gave birth to Jesus. In Mark 6:2-3 it says, And on the Sabbath he began to teach in the synagogue, and many who heard Him were astonished, saying, "Where did this man get these things? What is the wisdom given to him? How are such mighty works done by His hands? Is not this the carpenter, the son of Mary and brother of James and Joses and Judas Simon? And are not His sisters here with us?" And they took offense at Him. Matthew 13:53-57 gives this same account. The Apostle Paul in Galatians 1:19 says that when he first went to Jerusalem he did not see any of the disciples apart from Peter and James the Lord's brother. Mark 3:31 tells us of an occasion when His mother and brothers came to Him while he was teaching and the people in the crowd said to Jesus "Your mother and brothers are outside, seeking you."

I want to declare that I have great respect and appreciation for women. Therefore, I applaud those people who are bold enough to stand against all those men who use their power and position to sexually abuse women. Having said that, I want you to know that I'm totally against those in the "Me Too" movement who are joining the atheist and skeptics in mocking the God Christians worship.

Recently some people who represent the "Me Too" group, were seeking to undermine the Scripture. Some of the influential people in that movement have pushed back against the idea that God exists and this passage is one that is used to attack the Scripture and those who speak for God. I saw a picture recently which depicts the virgin Mary holding onto her belly and saying "Me Too." What they are trying to communicate is that God is a being who just abuses His power, and Mary has the evidence of pregnancy to prove it. It is so sad to observe that most times the skeptics and critics don't stop to read the account in the Scripture before they comment on it.

So, let us look at the account. First of all, you might notice that the Holy Spirit did not come up on Mary in a sexual manner as a man comes upon a woman sexually. The phrase "come up on" is used in Scripture for both male and female.

This is a common way of saying that the Holy Spirit is empowering God's servants for His service (Judges 14:6,19). This is true of the prophets as the Spirit of the Lord came upon them and they were able to perform works that they would not be able to do otherwise (Judges 14:6,19; 15:14).

Therefore, this was nothing sexual but it is the imagery of God overshadowing a temple in which He dwells to perform and show forth His glory like He did in the Tabernacle (Exodus 40:35). Notice that He says "The Holy Spirit will come upon you, and the power of the Most High will overshadow you" (Luke 1:35).

If they had taken the time to read the context and its connection, they would have understood that this was a fulfillment of a promise from the Old Testament (Isaiah 7:14). This prophecy is about the virgin who will be with child. But notice also that Mary was not just fearful in seeing the angel, she was also confused because she did not meet the normal requirements for being a mother. This is why she rightfully asked the question, "How can this be, since I am a virgin?" A man and a woman coming together in sexual intercourse is the normal way for a woman to get pregnant. But Mary had not had sex, so she was reasonably perplexed.

Now here is where the angel gave more information and clarified some things for her. The angel Gabriel explained to her that this is a divine intervention by the Holy Spirit. This is why the child shall be called the son of the Most High (Luke 1:32). He will also be given the throne of his father, David (Luke 1:33). It should be clear to us at this point that Jesus is both the Son of God and the son of David but not in the same sense. He is a descendant of David who has the rightful authority to rule on his throne and Jesus knew who He was even from childhood. One day, when he was inside the temple asking tough questions of the leaders, Mary and Joseph came to him and she said, "How could you do this to your father and I?" But Jesus sought to correct her gently by saying, "Did you not know that I must be in my Father's house?" (Luke 2:49).

Mary welcomed the will of God for her life when she said "Behold I am the servant of the Lord: let it be done to me according to your word" (Luke 1:38). This is a wonderful response that we all need to imitate. So that, when we hear the Lord's will for our lives, we make a total surrender and say like Mary, do as you please Lord, I am yours.

If the skeptics and the scoffers are insistent at mocking, then they should include me too. I join Mary in declaring that God has rescued *me too.* I was a sinner and He saved *me too.* Mary is saying she too has been blessed to be a blessing. I am not ashamed to say, *me too.* I have been redeemed and God can do the same for you too.

## Additional Questions to Ponder/Discuss

a. How do you understand the miraculous conception?
a. What would you think if your wife tells you that she is pregnant but she didn't have sex?
b. Are miracles possible today?

c. Do you believe that Jesus is the only Saviour? Why? Or why not?
d. Why does Mary need to be saved even though she carried the Saviour in her womb?

# PART 6: DEALING WITH COMMITMENT

# 19.
# Do you love me more than these? —John 21:15

## Prioritize Your Commitment

After Jesus was raised from the dead he showed himself to his disciples as they were fishing. Up until that time they were unsuccessful in catching any fish, and so Jesus told them to cast the net on the right side. As they did what he said they caught so many fish that they were not able to pull it in. However, when the disciples came to shore they realized that Jesus already had fish roasting on the fire. It was in that context that Jesus said to Peter "Simon son of John, do you love me more than these?" (John 21:15)

There are many theologians who have differing views on what the 'these' in the question asked in John 21: 15, "Do you love me more than these?" . Some say 'these' in this verse is referring to the fish that was caught. This is because Peter had left what Jesus had told him to do and had gone back to fishing. These scholars believe that the question was to serve as a rebuke.

Others say the word 'these' in the verse is referring to the other disciples. So, the question is, if Peter loves Jesus more than the other disciples. This they believe because Peter earlier was trying to prove that he was more committed to Jesus than all the rest (Mark 14:27-31.) For me, it does not matter if the word 'these' in the verse is referring to fish or other believers because whichever it is, the question is still, do you love Jesus more? If the question is about money, wife, husband, children or anything else, the question is still, do you love Jesus more?

Jesus then gave Peter work to do. In John 21:15-17, Jesus told Peter to feed His sheep. Jesus had already given them the Great Commission to make disciples of all nations. However, they seem to have taken a break from discipleship. Jesus had to remind Peter that there is no vacation from that vocation. The same is true for us today because the Great Commission is still our mission. Therefore, we cannot take a holiday from loving Jesus and serving Him. In John 14:15, Jesus says that if we love Him, we must keep His Commandments. That means to do what He says.

Mary said it well when she was trying to get Jesus to help a wedding feast that had run out of wine. She told the servants at the wedding "do whatever he tells you to do" (John 2:5). This is a word we too can embrace because if we do what He says we must do, He will do what only He can do.

As we examine ourselves, let us consider this question: do I love Jesus more than anything? More than anyone? If so, I must be about the Lord's business. Jesus already had fish and bread laid out for them, but he asked them, "Children, do you have any fish?" (John 21:5). Since they had left the Master's work to seek after fish, this could be a rebuke because they were acting immaturely. Note, Jesus has what you and I are searching for. What we need to do is love Him, seek Him and Serve him. Remember, whatever we need for true satisfaction can only be found in Him.

## Additional Questions to Ponder/Discuss

a. How can you tell if you love Jesus more than anything and anyone?
b. How can we be better prepared to share our faith?
c. When was the last time you won someone to the Lord?
d. Why did the disciples forsake the task that Jesus gave them?
e. Are you burdened for lost people to come to Christ?

# 20.
# Do you still hold fast to your integrity? —Job 2:9

## When It Hurts so Bad

Some time ago I heard about a little boy who was reading a story in which the villain was wreaking havoc in the community. The boy could not read any further because he became so afraid of what the villain would do next. He then turned to the back of the book and he read how the story ended. He turned back to where he stopped reading and every time, he saw the villain doing his evil acts, the boy would just smile and say, "Don't worry, I know how the story ends." When we read how the story ends at the back of our Bible, we can be confident that in the end, we win!

The story of Job in Scripture is very important because it gives us some insight into the problem of pain and suffering. It is a book that seeks to answer both the emotional and the intellectual problem of pain. It also helps to clear up some wrong assumptions about who suffers. Some people, including Job's three friends who came to visit him during his ordeal, believe that God does not allow the righteous to suffer. Right at the beginning of the story we are told that Job was a righteous man who revered God and shunned evil (Job 1:1). Job was not perfect in the sense of being sinless, but he was an upright man with no double life or hypocrisy. This is the reason so many people ask the question why they experience pain and suffering. If he were an evil man who seeks to cause pain and destruction in the life of others, we would assume that he would reap what he sowed. But when one lives good and then bad things happen, it seems to be unfair.

Job lost his wealth, his health, his children and his servants, but he did not lose his sanity. It is one thing for pain to come into our lives but when it comes suddenly and unexpectedly, it impacts us even more. His problems did not only happen suddenly, but they came with great severity (Job 1:13-19). Now the source of Job's pain and suffering was not because of his sin, it was because Satan wanted to destroy his love and trust in God. Satan wanted to show that Job was not sincere in his commitment to God. He thought Job was just serving God for what he could get (Job 1:9-11). God knew that Satan wanted to bring disaster to destroy Job and everything belonging to Job so that he might turn away from Him. Although Satan meant it for evil, God allowed it for good. It is good that God has lifted the curtains of heaven and has given us a glimpse of what took place (Job 1: 6-8). This is similar to how God allowed Joseph to suffer greatly at the hands of his brothers and be sold into slavery because He had a plan to use their evil for His good (Genesis 50:20).

Job's wife wanted him to curse God and die because she thought that God was being cruel to her husband. She could not understand why Job was still being steadfast in his faith.. She asked, "Do you still hold fast to your integrity?" (Job 2:9) Many people are tempted to walk away from the Lord when they suffer. They can't see why a loving God would allow pain and suffering in their life. We need to remember that His ways are higher than ours. He is infinite and we are finite (Isaiah 55:89). One of my favorite lecturers at seminary, Dr. Delano Palmer used to say, "God is wise, and we are otherwise."

Pain can take us to a place of madness. This is why the problem is not just an intellectual problem but an emotional one. Notice the madness coming out of Mrs. Job's pain, "Curse God and die" (Job 2:9). So when we seek to help people in their suffering, don't reason like Job's friends Zophar, Bildad and Eliphaz or like his wife. If you don't have anything good to say, then keep silent and you will communicate more care. His friends did better while they stayed with him for days and said nothing.

I once heard of a story which gives an example of how we human beings sometimes cannot understand what God is doing when he allows pain into our lives. It is about a bear who was caught in a trap in the forest. A man tried to help the bear, but the bear thought he was trying to hurt him. To rescue the bear, he had to shoot him with a dose of tranquilizer to get him to sleep. While the man was taking the bear out, there was too much pressure on the trap, so he had to push the bear further into the trap cage to release the tension. If the bear had gained consciousness at that point, he would be even more convinced that the man wanted to hurt him. Now the bear would feel this way because he does not understand what the man is doing. Could this be true for us as well, that because we don't understand what God is doing, we think that He is trying to hurt us?

The book of Job is littered with the question why because Job wanted answers about his suffering and great pain. However, when God responded to Job it seems to be a rebuke to Job for demanding that God answer his concerns. In the last five chapters of the book God showed Job who He is, that He is the Sovereign Lord and Creator of the universe (Job 38-42).

Then Job responded in awe and repentance and a change of perspective. What happened? What caused the change? God showed Himself as the answer to our suffering. God did not give him some writing in the sky to explain but He showed Job that He is the awesome God of heaven who cares for people on earth.

Whenever you are tempted to think that God is up in heaven and ignoring and avoiding your pain and suffering, just look back at Calvary. God doesn't always just give us answers to our problems. He is the answer to our problems. When Job saw the Savior, he was satisfied, and we will too when we take a look at Jesus on the cross. God left the splendor of heaven and took on a human body so that He could enter our pain (Phil. 2:6-10).

It will soon be over, all troubles and trials, when God makes all things new. The apostle John concurs with that fact in Revelation 21:3-4. The text says that all our pain and suffering will come to an end. However, while we wait, let's hold fast to our integrity. "Be steadfast and unmovable, always abounding in the work of the Lord, knowing that your labor in the Lord is not in vain" (1Corinthians 15:58). For the things we now suffer are not worthy to be compared with what we will receive (Romans 8:18). Paul referred to all his suffering as light affliction in light of God's eternal weight of glory (2Corinthians 4:17). I know the problem of pain and suffering is not easy, but I implore you, trust God, because unlike that helpless bear, we know that God cares.

## Additional Questions to Ponder/Discuss

a. How do you feel about God when you are suffering?
b. Why did Job hold on to his integrity?
c. What do you think about Job's wife's suggestion to curse God and die?
d. Should we ask God to tell us why we are going through suffering? If not, why not?
e. When God is silent, do you still believe that He is present in your situation?

# 21.
# How can a young man keep his way pure? —Psalm 119:9

## Purity pays

Keeping our way pure is something that we must do with the help of the Holy Spirit in our life. But the question is, how can it be done? We are given a jumpstart in answering this question right in this very text in Psalm 119:9-11. Psalm 119 stresses the importance of the word of God in our lives. Verses 9-11 says How can a young man keep his way pure? By guarding it according to your word. With my whole heart I seek you; let me not wander from your commandments! I have stored up your word in my heart, that I might not sin against you. It says that we must guard our heart always with God's word. This involves studying the word of God and storing it up in our hearts that we might not sin against God. This can be accomplished by meditating on the word of God and delighting ourselves in it.

If we are going to keep our way pure, we have to set our affections on the things of God and not on the world (Colossians 3:12). This, we are exhorted to do because we are new people in Christ. Those who are in Christ have been made new. So, we should therefore glorify God with our body which belongs to God (2Corinthians 5:17). The most important thing to possess that will help us to keep our way pure is the knowledge of who we are and whose we are.

Many years ago, I heard a story about a young eaglet that fell from its nest. He grew up among some turkeys who nurtured him and taught him how to live. Then one day he saw an eagle in the sky who then came down and asked him "What are you doing down here?" The little eagle told him that he had lived there all his life. The wise eagle told him to begin to flap his wing and as he did, he began to fly. At that time one of the turkeys began to shout, "Where are you going, what are you going to do? Who do you think you are?" When the little eagle was rising to the sky he shouted, "I'm going where I belong and I'm going to live the way I'm supposed to because I am an eagle you turkey!"

Sometimes Christians find themselves living a compromised life which does not present a good witness for Christ. These believers usually get that "turkey" response when they decide to leave that low lifestyle and start to fully surrender to the Spirit of God. Your friends will say ,"You have walked, eaten and slept with us, you went to the same places and watched and listened to the same things as us, what has gotten into you, who do you think you are?" At this point you need to remember who you are and say it.

When we recognize that we are saints in Christ and that we have been bought with a price and we don't belong to ourselves, we cannot live the same way we used to (1Corinthians 6:19-20). Seeking God and storing up His words in our heart is the starting point to keeping our way pure, but that's not all. It takes more than storing up God's word in our hearts to remain pure because we have an enemy whose aim is to kill, steal and destroy us, (John 10:10). We have some fighting to do if we are going to live pure.

The devil shoots fiery darts at us; darts of deception and lies that will cause us to hate and covet and fight our family and friends while thinking that they are the enemy. But we are not left hopeless or helpless because the Holy Spirit dwells within us. Remember that this war is not against flesh and blood, but against spiritual wickedness in heavenly places (Ephesians 6:12-13). The Lord knows that the devil has weapons, so He has equipped us with weapons as well. These weapons must be worn daily because without them we are not able to win. The only way we will be victorious is if we stand in the power of God and not in our own strength (Ephesians 6:10). For it is God who is at work in us to will and to do of His good pleasure (Philippians 2:13). The power to withstand or resist the devil doesn't come from us but only from the Holy Spirit and flows through us.

We are told in James chapter four that if we submit ourselves to God then we can resist the devil and he will flee from us. James exhorts us to draw near to God and He will draw near to us (James 4:6-8). Please don't miss this important point. If there is no humility and submission to

God, then there is no power to resist the devil. There is a classic example of this truth demonstrated in the life of Samson. Samson trusted in his own strength and thought that he could just do as he pleased and still have the power to defeat the enemy. But the Scripture says that when Samson stood up to fight those who came to take him captive, he had no power and he did not realize that the Lord had left him (Judges 16:20).

Now I know that believers today are indwelt by the Holy Spirit of God and He doesn't come and go when we fall. But the point I'm trying to make here is that if we are not depending on God, we won't even realize when we are fighting on our own, and that is a scary thing to attempt against our enemy, the devil. So, let us not fool ourselves like Samson, thinking we are self-sufficient, because that's what the devil wants us to believe. Please remember that our sufficiency is in Christ. Let me make one last point here. Don't be like the lady who said, "My mom hid my dolly in her trunk, that is why I'm always drunk." Don't be afraid to own your failures or mistakes. Don't blame anyone. Instead, confess it, repent and continue to guard your way. Will you keep your way pure today? You have the power to do it.

## Additional Questions to Ponder/Discuss

a. What are the benefits of living pure?
b. How are you doing in your spiritual warfare?

c. Do you have an accountable partner who helps you to keep focused?
d. List some steps that you have taken to live pure?
e. How can we become alert to the Devil's schemes?

# 22.
# Are we to continue in sin that grace may abound? —Romans 6:1

## Understanding Grace

Many people misunderstand what the Scriptures teach about grace. This has been happening from ancient times. In Romans 6:1 Paul asks "Are we to continue in sin that grace may abound?" In this context the Apostle Paul sought to explain the greatness of God's amazing grace. In the previous chapters in Romans Paul explained the problem of sin and its consequences. He showed how God made a way to pay the price for our sin and offer us salvation.

Paul asked, "Are we to continue in sin that grace may abound?" He asked the question in anticipation of some person's misuse or misunderstanding of his preaching on grace. Paul had earlier told them that where sin increased, grace increased even more (Romans 5:30). In light of this fact some people think that grace gives them a license to sin. This is a dreadful misunderstanding of grace. If a man is granted grace after he has committed a crime, it is not to encourage him to continue in his criminality. So that kind of reasoning is just ridiculous. This is why Paul responded to it with such strong words. Paul used the Greek words "Me genoito", which the ESV translates as "By no means!" But the strength of his response to today's listeners would be like saying, "Are you crazy?" or "What kind of thinking is that?"

Acts of willful sin will bring punishment and that wasn't what Paul wanted for his readers. He was emphasizing the greatness of God's grace in order that they would respond with loving obedience and gratitude (Romans 12:1-2). Paul is saying that it does not make any sense for someone who has died to sin to continue to live in the pleasure of sin (Romans 6:2-3). We now have a new experience in a new relationship which gives us a new identity that we might live in a new way.

Let us look briefly at the new experience. This new experience is that we have died to sin when we trusted Jesus for salvation. This is about identification. So, when you placed your faith in Christ' atoning sacrifice for your sin, that payment was applied to your account even though you did not actually pay anything. You are now alive to Christ and dead to sin. That means we are now united with Christ.

We also share a new relationship with Christ. When we were in the world, we were considered to be enemies and outsiders but now we are friends and children of God. We are also called co-workers with God as it pertains to His agenda of reaching the lost (1 Corinthians 3:9). Paul tells us that now that we have been justified by faith, we have peace with God (Romans 5:1). We are children of God through faith (1 John 3:1-3; Galatians 3:26).

Our new identity is that we are saints in Christ (1 Corinthians 1:2). We are the righteousness of God in Christ. Therefore, the significance of our new identity is found in Christ and not in ourselves (2 Corinthians 5:21). The apostle Paul wanted the believers at Corinth to be saints in their lifestyle because they were already saints in their position in Christ. Paul beseeches the brethren to live differently because they were different.

The fact is that there is a struggle going on in our body and mind that seeks to prevent us from living consistently Christ-like. Paul said that when he wanted to do good, he actually did what was bad. He was losing the battle at this time in his life because he was trying to live the life of God. But this is not possible because the Christian life cannot be lived in our own strength or according to our flesh. Paul saw the futility of trying to accomplish this and cried out for help. He found the victory in yielding to Christ and allowing the Holy Spirit to live through him (Romans 7:24-25). It was a shout of triumph when he was set free from himself.

The final area in which we are new is in our lifestyle. Paul gives us some tips as to how we can live differently. He says that it takes reckoning. That is, we must consider or count to be true the fact that we are now in Christ and that we are not the same people we used to be (Romans 6:11). We must not allow the deeds of the old lifestyle to take root in our life. Nor should we allow our body to be used as instruments of unrighteousness; because sin must not dominate us, since we have been set free by the grace of God (Romans 6:12-14).

There are many negative consequences for a believer who takes grace for granted. In the Corinthian church there was a young man who was sleeping with his father's wife and he was disciplined by the church after Paul instructed them to put him out of fellowship (1Corinthians 5:1-11). There were also some people who were treating the communion with disdain and disregard and some of them died and others got sick as an account of discipline from God (1Corinthians 11:27-31). Paul lets us know that those who don't build well on the foundation they have received (this foundation is Christ) will suffer loss of their reward (1Corinthians 3:9-14). Remember we will all stand before God to give an account for the life we live (2 Corinthians 5:10).

Paul says in Galatians 5:16, "Walk by the Spirit, and you will not gratify the desires of the flesh. This does not mean that we will not have any bad desires, it only means that those bad desires will not have us. If we keep our mind on the right things, we will be able to resist the temptations. Paul says in Galatians "Whatever things are true, honorable, just, pure, lovely, and commendable think on these things "(Philippians 4:8). The most important thing is to live right and to yield ourselves to God. The Bible says submit yourself to God and resist the devil and he will flee (James 4:6-7

The thing that will help us to not abuse God's grace, is to remember where we are coming from. Paul asked the believers if they had benefited from their life of sin. His question is that, since it did not profit them, why would they want to go back to living in sin and abuse the grace of God? (Romans 6:19-23). In light of God's mercy towards you, present your body to him in total surrender.

## Additional Questions to Ponder/Discuss

a. Why do some Christians abuse God's grace?
b. Does God tempt us to sin?
c. What is the key to living the Christian life?
d. What are we to do when we are tempted?
e. List four things about your new identity?

# 23.

# Do you want to go away as well? —John 6:67

## The Cost of Discipleship

When our faith is tested by the purifying work of the Holy Spirit and the word of God, we need to submit. On one occasion Jesus was speaking to his disciples and the things he taught them were too harsh or uncomfortable for them to accept. John 6 tells us that when Jesus told the people that he is The Bread from heaven that the Father has given to the world, and unless they eat of His flesh and drink of his blood they cannot have eternal life, many people, including some his followers were offended. Therefore, many of them walked away from Jesus and stopped following him.

In this context, Jesus made it clear that not everyone is seeking him for who He is. Some people are seeking Jesus for what they received or for the temporal blessing (John 6:26). Some people came to Jesus, but the moment things got hard or uncomfortable they walked away. They were deluded into thinking that being Jesus' disciple meant that he would just give them what they wanted, and life would be easy. The moment shame or persecution comes because of their association with Christ or the claims of Christ, they stop following Jesus.

Many people today are in a similar position. They want to be a disciple, but they are not prepared to deal with the discrimination, disdain or disrespect that come with identifying with Jesus. These are the persons who get easily offended and fall away. This type of desertion however, will not happen if we remain focused on the offer Jesus gives. He said, "Come unto me all who are tired and weary and I will give you rest" (Matthew 11:29-30). But we can only experience this rest if we take His yoke and be taught and guided by Him.

In John chapter 6:35 Jesus said to them "I am the bread of life; whoever believes in me shall not hunger, and whoever believes in me shall never thirst". He continued in verse 51 where he said "I am the living bread that came down from heaven. If anyone eats of this bread, he will live forever. And the bread that I will give for the life of the world is my flesh". Jesus was not encouraging cannibalism when He told them that unless they eat of His flesh and drink of His blood they will not have life, He was speaking metaphorically. Should anyone believe that when he or she participates in communion today, the emblem of bread and wine actually becomes Jesus' literal flesh and blood? No! Notice the analogy of food for the body. Unless we receive food and drink for our bodies, we will die. In the same way, if we don't receive Jesus, who is the bread from heaven, then we will die in our sins, (John 6:41).

Jesus is the manna that the Father gives (John 6:30-33). The point being made by Jesus is that if we come to know Him as our Saviour, then we will know life. If we reject Jesus, we will not come to know life eternal. The Apostle John tells us in 1John 5:12, "Whoever has the Son has life; whoever does not have the Son of God does not have life." It is good to see that some people are already convinced that there is no one else to go to if they are to get eternal life. Therefore, Peter responded with a question, "Lord, to whom shall we go?" (John 6:68). Peter admits that Jesus is the source of eternal life.

Everybody needs someone to lean on sometimes. Everybody needs somewhere to run to sometimes. But friends may leave us when times are tough, family might abandon us when things get rough, finance might finish when we are really in need, but Jesus is The Rock in whom we can hide. He is a shelter to which we can run. He promises never to leave us or forsake us (Hebrews 13:5). This assurance and comfort is given many times in Scripture because God wants us to remember it. "Do not be afraid for the Lord your God goes with you, He will never leave you nor forsake you" (Deuteronomy 31:6). So, when we are tempted to walk away from Jesus Christ, we can say with confidence that there is nowhere else to go, He alone is eternal life. I know that the cost of living today is high, but I know the cost of leaving Christ is higher. So, hold on brethren though things may be tough, remember He is holding on to you.

## Additional Questions to Ponder/Discuss

a. What is the cost of discipleship?
b. Have you ever felt like walking away from Jesus?
c. What led you to think that it is better to stay with Jesus?
d. Do you face ridicule for your faith in Jesus?
e. How can a person experience God's rest?

# 24.

# What is that to you?

# —John 21:22

## Stay Focused on Jesus

Peter turned and saw the disciple whom Jesus loved following them, the one who had been reclining at the table close to him and had said, "Lord, who is it that is going to betray you?" 21. When Peter saw him he said to Jesus, Lord what about this man?" Jesus said to him, "If it is my will that he remain until I come, what is that to you? You follow me!" So, the saying spread abroad among the brothers that this disciple was not to die; yet Jesus did not say to him that he was not to die, but, "If it is my will that he remain until I come, what is that to you?" (John 21:20-23)

There was a rumor going around during the time when Jesus walked with His disciples after He was raised from the dead. The rumor was that Jesus said that one of His disciples wouldn't die until He returns. However, Jesus did not say that, what Jesus said to Peter is, if he wills that the disciple remains until he comes back it's not Peter's business. It seems that Peter had made it his business. I wonder who started the rumor. Anyway, let us not start calling names.

Peter was speaking what God says when he said that Jesus is the Christ, the son the living God (Matthew 16:16). He then began to speak for Satan when he objected to Jesus going to the cross (Matthew 16:22-23). It doesn't matter how much theology we have, if we don't embrace the way of the cross in our preaching and lifestyle, it amounts to nothing.

Peter was happy with the fame of Jesus, while rejecting the mission of Jesus. Jesus came to seek and save the lost (Luke 19:10). The crowd was growing, and people were being healed and that was sufficient for Peter. He could do without the suffering and shame and death, but we cannot have the true Christ without it. We can't have real salvation without it. Nor can we be true disciples of Christ without bearing our own cross. We can declare who Christ is by means of revelation, but we will only follow him by means of our submission and dedication. It's not just about proclaiming the cross, it's also about growing in Christ.

Jesus told them about the reality of the cost. In Luke 9:23 Jesus said, "If anyone would come after me, let him deny himself and take up his cross daily and follow me." Jesus wants us to do more than just listen to His teaching, He wants real students who are learning and adopting the master's ways. Peter, like many Christians today, was focused on dying for Jesus, but Jesus wants some more people who are willing to live for him.

According to Jesus, if we die to self, we can live for Him. A person can have a desire to follow Christ, and also to follow through on that desire. Jesus doesn't just tell them about the reality of the cost, but also about the reason for the cost. He said that without paying the cost they cannot be His disciples. Let me be clear, that I'm not suggesting that we can pay for salvation, I'm saying that we must bear the shame and persecution that come with following Jesus. The reason for the cost is that we might be like Jesus. In Matthew we are told "A disciple is not above his teacher, nor a servant above his master" (Matthew 10:25). There is also a reward for bearing the cost. In John 15:5 it says that those who abide or walk in obedience to Christ will bear much fruit. But the rewards for faithfulness go beyond this life. If we follow Christ closely, one day He will say to us, Well done, good and faithful servant and give us eternal rewards according to our works.

After Jesus told Peter how he was going to suffer, Peter immediately looked at John and asked Jesus what is going to happen to John, but Jesus said "If it is my will that he remains until I come, what is that to you? You follow me!" (John 21:22). The question that Jesus asked Peter is relevant to us today, because we sometimes fall into the same situation as Peter. For example, we get caught up looking and listening to what God is doing in the life of another person and begin to compare it with what God is doing in our own life. This sometimes leads to jealousy, because we believe that God is doing more for them than He is doing for us. If we are not careful, we might develop an attitude of ingratitude.

Jesus told Peter to stop focusing on what He is doing with John because He wants Peter to focus and follow Him. So yes, you have been saved and you see God doing tremendous things through other ministers, so much that they are well recognized by many people. They also seem to have little or no troubles. Jesus is asking the question, "What is that to you? Follow me." Some might have been serving at the school or work and even church and some persons have been promoted who came after you. You have no grievance against those who have been promoted, but still you want to know why God would allow you to remain at the same place while they are promoted. It now seems like another season of blessing is in their life and you are asking how come? Jesus is still asking, "What is that to you? Follow me."

## Additional Questions to Ponder/Discuss

a. What are some of the possible implications if we focus on others instead of Jesus?
b. Have you ever lost focus on Christ?
c. What are the benefits of having your heart fixed on Jesus?
d. What does Isaiah 26:3 say about keeping focused?

e. What did you learn from how that rumor got started?

# 25.
# How long will you go limping between two opinions?
# —1 Kings 18:21

## Ambivalence Keeps Us on the Fence

In 1 Kings 18 we read the story of how the people of God had wandered away from their commitment to Him. Many of them were ambivalent and double minded in their approach towards God. Here is where we pick up the reading in verse 20. So Ahab sent to all the people of Israel and gathered the prophets together at Mount Carmel. 21. And Elijah came near to all the people and said, "How long will you go limping between two different opinions? If the Lord is God, follow him; but if Baal, then follow him"

One of the surest things I have learned is that you can't run your race on the sidelines, nor can you win the race by staying on the fence. The people of God at this time were not steadfast in their commitment to God and God, through His prophet Elijah caused a great drought in the land. King Ahab was fed up with having Elijah around and alive in the country. He claimed that Elijah was the cause of all Israel's problems, so he called Elijah a troublemaker (1 Kings 18:17). He said this because Elijah had prophesied that there would be a drought in the land, and it came to pass.

The country was struggling because their crops and livestock were dying, and this caused great suffering to the people. Therefore, King Ahab saw Elijah as a stumbling block to his regime. Elijah on the other hand saw king Ahab and his family as a stumbling block and troubler of Israel (v.18). This is because they had abandoned the commandments of the Lord and followed other gods (v.18). So, Elijah was also fed up with Ahab and the people who were treating God with disdain.

Elijah wanted the people to be sincere. He was tired of people sitting on the fence as it pertains to serving the true God. He asked them, "How long will you go limping between two opinions?" (1 Kings 18:21). His passion for God was evident here because he wanted people to stop playing around with God. We see the same thing in our society today when great calamity strikes. Some people call out to God, but as soon as things are back to normal, they return to serving self and sin. Elijah is saying, *come on people, it's either we know God and serve Him, or we don't.*

In order to settle this state of ambivalence among the people, Elijah gave them a challenge to prove who is the real God. He offered a bull and the prophets of Baal also offered a bull and whichever God answered by bringing down fire on the altar would be declared the real God. The king and the people along with false prophets agreed with the terms of the challenge. The false prophets were allowed to go first but their god could not answer by fire. Therefore, Elijah mocked and teased them, telling them to cry louder because their god might be gone to the restroom. The prophets of Baal began to cut themselves so that their blood gushed out (1 Kings 18: 27-29). This they believe, would invoke the intervention of the gods.

There is some resemblance of this in today's society. Some people are trying to get supernatural intervention by doing harm to themselves. That type of practice is demonic. It did not work well then and it does not work well for individuals now.

Back to the story. It was now Elijah's turn and he started by praying and praising God (1 Kings 18:30-37). The Lord then answered by fire and consumed the offering. Something amazing happened here that we must not miss. God also caused the wood that was soaking wet to be consumed. Elijah was putting himself at a disadvantage when he wetted the wood, but he was confident that he would win the challenge, because God was his advantage to win. This demonstration of the power of God caused the people to be struck with awe and cry out that the Lord is truly God (v 38-39). The false prophets were then destroyed for all the harm they had brought to the nation.

There are a couple important things I want to point out here. Notice that the people's hearts were not on fire for God but the servant of the Lord played his role in bringing them to their senses. He challenged them about their lack of commitment to the true God and made it clear that it is useless to run after other gods. Elijah also repaired the altar of the Lord that had been broken down and neglected for so long.

We too have a role to play in bringing people to their senses and turning them to God. That can only happen if, like Elijah, we have a passion for God. Elijah was not seeking glory for himself, he wanted the people to worship God. We can do this by letting our light shine before men that as they see our good works they will come to know and love God (Matthew 5:16). If we have somehow been neglecting our personal quiet time and intimacy with God, we need to repair that alter. If we have been going to church out of mere formality or tradition, then the Lord demands more than that.

The only thing that will keep us at the altar of the true and living God is our love for Him, which must be manifested in our loyalty to Jesus. Our duty must come from a heart of devotion and intimacy with God. Are you playing your role in God's kingdom agenda or are you wavering between two opinions?

## Additional Questions to Ponder/Discuss

a. Was it fitting for Elijah to be upset over their double mindedness?
b. What are the implications of constant wavering?
c. Why does it pay to be sincere?

d. How can Christians be more effective in defending their Christian worldview?
e. Why is it important to be able to give an answer to those who ask why you are a Christian?

# PART 7:

# DEALING WITH DISOBEDIENCE AND DECEIT

# 26.
# Why do you call me Lord, Lord and not do what I tell you? —Luke 6:46

## The Value of Obedience

Why do you call me Lord, Lord, and not do what I tell you? Everyone who comes to me and hears my words and does them, I will show you what he is like: He is like a man building a house, who dug deep and laid the foundation on the rock. And when a flood arose, the stream broke against that house and could not shake it, because it had been well built. But the one who hears and does not do them is like a man who built a house on the ground without foundation. When the stream broke against it, immediately it fell, and the ruin of that house was great (Luke 6:46-49)

For many years I have listened to messages on this particular portion of Scripture. Almost all the preaching or teaching are usually centered on having a good foundation which is then defined to be Jesus Christ. I will agree that there are a couple places in Scripture where Jesus is referred to as a Rock or as a foundation. However, it is important to note that this portion is not about Jesus being our foundation. The emphasis of the passage is to explain the importance of obedience.

Jesus, as he taught on this occasion, used word pictures to demonstrate what happens in an obedient life in contrast to what happens in a life lived in pretense and disobedience. Notice that both houses faced the same trials. Both houses may even look the same on the outside. The difference was realized when the storm came. Although Jesus' teaching here gives us good advice on building construction, well at least some areas in construction, the text is not about how to construct a house, but about being obedient to the truth of God's word.

Jesus was only showing us what a person who obeys God looks like. He is like a person who built his house on the rock. As believers, if we don't build our lives on God's word by applying it, the storms of life will get the better of us. Notice that truth is applicable even to two Christians who might be building their lives on different things. This passage is not dealing with what happens to the unsaved versus what happens to the saved. It is simply discussing the importance of obedience. For example, two Christians might be going through the same storm in life, but one is falling apart, while the other is still standing in spite of the storm. One is still obeying God, while the other has thrown in the towel and is walking away from God.

We need to remember that before Jesus gave the story about the two houses, he asked an important question. The question was, "Why do you call me Lord, Lord and not do what I tell you?" (Luke 6:46). The idea that is communicated in this question is that these people are living in pretense; they say one thing with their mouth but they reject the truth of God for their life. Therefore, the question of why people do that can only be answered personally. However, I believe the primary reason we do that is because we want others to think of us highly. This describes many of the religious leaders at that time. God knows who we are and how we are so there is no need for pretense. We are exhorted to "Be doers of the word and not hearers only, deceive ourselves" (James 1:22).

The issue of obedience comes up again in Matthew 21:28-31. Jesus told a story of a father who told both of his sons to go and work in his vineyard. The first son said *no* but later repented and went to work in the field. The second son promised to go but he didn't. Jesus asked the people to tell him what they thought about who actually obeyed the father; they said the first son.

It may be that we have said yes to God our Father about working in his field, but we have not followed through on that. It's not too late for us to start today. Or maybe you had said *no, it is too hard, it takes too much of your precious time.* If that describes you, you too can repent and start doing the Father's will by going out into His field. If we refuse to surrender in obedience to the Lord, why then do we continue to call him Lord?

## Additional Questions to Ponder/Discuss

a. Can we measure our spiritual maturity outside of obedience?
b. If obedience determines one's spirituality, how spiritual are you?
c. What does James 1:22-25 mean by the *forgetful hearer*?
d. What was Jesus' purpose for telling this story?
e. How does obedience help us in the storms of life?

# 27.
# Is this not the fast that I have chosen? —Isaiah 58: 6

## Getting Fasting Right

Fasting is one of the spiritual disciplines in Christianity that many people practice, but some are not very aware of the real purpose of fasting. Fasting is done for various reasons and by different groups. It is done for dietary reasons by people who are focused on their health. Some people fast for political reasons as well as when they want to make a point or stand against a group or government. I want to focus our attention on fasting that takes place for religious reasons.

Fasting is the practice of abstaining from food for a specified period. This is why we are warned in Matthew 6:16-18 where Jesus said "And when you fast, do not look gloomy like the hypocrites, for they disfigure their faces that their fasting may be seen to others. Truly I say to you, they have received their reward. But when you fast, anoint your head and wash your face, that your fasting may not be seen by others but by your Father who is in secret. And your Father who sees in secret will reward you." Therefore, we must not fast to be seen by men because if we do, we will not be rewarded by our Father in heaven. The point Jesus is making in the text is not that we must not be seen fasting but that we must not fast to be seen.

Fasting in the Bible was practiced even among people of different nations who worshipped other gods (Jonah 3:5-10). The people of God usually fast when they are in difficult and desperate situations such as in Esther chapter 4. It was also done at a time when one needed insight and energy for the battle ahead (Esther 4:15-16). In both of the texts mentioned, we read about how the people were in a serious situation that could cost them their lives.

Jesus fasted in the desert for forty days and nights but He still had to face his trials and temptations (Matthew 4:1-11). He spent quality intimate time with His heavenly Father but he still had to face the cross. (Matthew 26:36-46) This is important to understand, because fasting is not a tool to keep trouble or trials from coming in our lives. Rather, it's a means by which we remain humble and submissive to the will of our Heavenly Father. It is primarily about intimacy with God and less about material gains from Him. the people all participated and God showed them mercy because they repented (Jonah 3:10).

Fasting in Bible times was also often done at a place or time of mourning. However, today many fast for the purpose of dieting. Although it is good to be fit, the purpose of fasting in the Scriptures is not to be healthy or happy but it is to be holy. Neither our fasting nor our faith obligates God to act in the way we want. This is why some people do not gain anything from fasting and so they become discouraged and disheartened. Fasting is not meant for us to get God to do what we want, but it is to get us at a place of humility, so we will do what He wants.

Some practice lengthy periods of fasting because they believe that it is the length of their fasting that determines the strength of their fasting. We should be cognizant of the fact that our fasting cannot force God's hand. It does not make God want what we want.

God sought to address the issue of fasting by explaining to His people about the type of fast that He desires. In Isaiah 58 the people were only going through the motions and dealing with fasting in a legalistic way while still living a sinful lifestyle (Isaiah 58:1-4). They were praising God with their lips but their hearts were far from him. God rejected their fast because they focused on the art of fasting, while hating people in their heart (v 4-5).

The description in these verses indicate that these people would punish themselves while fasting because they believed that it would earn God's approval. They thought that if the fasting hurt, then it would work, but that is not true. The only pain that we need to experience in fasting is that which comes by humbling ourselves before God and denying our fleshly desires. That will cause our carnal man to cry out because our body is not being used as an instrument of unrighteousness. The Apostle Paul implores us in Romans to put to death the deeds of the flesh and yield to the Spirit of God (Romans 6:12-14).

In Isaiah 58:6-7 God broadens the scope by giving us insight into the areas of fasting. For example, He tells us that the fasting that He has chosen is one that puts away evil by refusing to fight against others and having a hateful attitude towards people. Not only to put away evil but to promote what is good. To loose the bands of wickedness, to take the heavy burdens from people, to let the oppressed go free, to share with those who are hungry and to care for the less fortunate who are without clothes and shelter (Isaiah 58:6-7).

Therefore, the next time we plan to fast, just remember that the fast that God has chosen is not only denying food from entering our body, but denying sin from dominating our lives. We may need to fast from some Social Media, some things on television or some music that is making it difficult for us to keep our bodies under subjection. Remember the old saying, "rubbish in, rubbish out." Will you engage in the fast that God has chosen?

## Additional Questions to Ponder/Discuss

a. Is fasting important for Christians today?
b. What does fasting accomplish in the life of the believer?
c. Why do people believe that the length of the fast determines the strength of it?

d. Why did Jesus say that we must not fast to be seen by men?
e. Should we still fast if we are practicing sin?

# 28.
# Is not my word like fire and like a hammer? —Jeremiah 23:29

## Be True to God's Word

"Behold, I am against those who prophesy lying dreams, declares the Lord, and who tell them and lead my people astray by their lies and their recklessness, when I did not send them or charge them. So they do not profit this people at all, declares the Lord" (Jeremiah 23:32).

The warning in this text is very relevant to us today because much of what was happening in the religious arena then, is happening now. In Jeremiah 23, God commanded the people not to listen to the false prophets. They were deceiving the people by giving them false hope and telling them what they wanted to hear (v.17). They told the people that there is no consequence for their sins. Therefore, the people could live any way they pleased (v.17). These prophets were not coming before God to listen to Him and to hear from God. Therefore, they could not be speaking on God's behalf because God did not speak to them (v.18.) The Lord made it clear that contrary to what the false prophet said, He would punish sin and all disobedience (v. 19-20).

These prophets were not sent by God, but they went under the guise of representing God because it would give them some amount of credential with the people. Many false prophets today are doing the same thing. They are preaching their dreams, wishes and desires instead of God's words. This was what caused God to be angry with the prophets. God said to them that they may speak to the people, but don't call His name. He wanted them to be true in what they were doing.

He says if the prophet has a word that he wants to tell the people, he should do so, but don't say that God said it because God did not say it (v. 21). The false prophets were holding back the people by keeping the truth of God from them. Here is something interesting, the Lord said that if the false prophet had stood in His council and preached the truth of His word, then the people would have turned from their evil ways (v 22). These prophets were holding revival, but God wanted a true preacher to set the revival loose. It means therefore, that we must be careful to learn and to live the teachings of God's word, so people may see our good works and glorify our Father in heaven (Matthew 5:16).

God explained to them that He sees and knows everything, so nothing that is done in the dark is hidden from Him (Jerimiah 23:23-25). The lesson here is that we must seek to make disciples for Christ and not for ourselves. We don't need to have a great following for ourselves, but we need to lead people to follow Christ. Jesus says in Matthew 28:19, "Go therefore and make disciples of all nations, baptizing them in the name of the Father and the Son and the Holy Spirit."

Look at how the Lord compared the words of the false prophets to His words. God asks, "What is the straw in comparison to the grain?" (v. 28). Here God is saying that the straw looks good or sounds good, but it lacks real substance. He is likening His word to fire and a hammer, both of which have the power to create an impact for change (v.29).

Finally, we must seek to preach the truth of God's word in season or out of season; when people want to hear and when they don't want to hear (2Timothy 4:2). For some will not put up with the sound teaching but will seek to get people to tell them what they want to hear. These people have the itchy ear syndrome. It is required for us that those who have been given a trust must be faithful (1Corinthians 4:2.) How are you treating God's words? Do remember, if the prophecy doesn't happen, then it wasn't God at all (Jeremiah 28:9; Deuteronomy 18:22). If God did not send you, don't say that He did.

## Additional Questions to Ponder/Discuss

a. Does a preacher's dream carry the same authority as the Scriptures?

b. Do you enjoy listening to humorous or fiery preaching, even if it's not scriptural?
c. How can we tell if someone is a prophet of God?
d. What value do you place on the Scriptures?
e. Do you spend more time listening to songs than to Scripture?

# 29.

# Is it lawful to pay taxes?

# —Mark 12:14

## God's Mark Is on You

During the time of Jesus on earth, the Romans were in control. They had power over the Jews, and their governing strategy was very oppressive. There were several different taxes and specific areas of collection. Since the Jews were being oppressed through these taxes, they despised any of their fellow Jews who worked for the Roman government as a tax collector. This is so because they are seen as agreeing with an oppressive system. No wonder someone like Zacchaeus was snarled at by the Jewish group who complained that Jesus would go to the home of a tax collector. They even despised Jesus for accepting a person like Zacchaeus. These Jewish tax collectors were not allowed into the synagogue or the temple or in the general religious arena, yet they were welcomed by Jesus. Jesus declared that he came to seek and to save the lost (Luke 19:6-10).

We are told in Mark 12:14 that the Pharisees and the Herodians tried to trap Jesus. It reads, "And they came and said to him, Teacher, we know that you are true and do not care about anyone's opinion. For you are not swayed by appearances, but truly teach the way of God. Is it lawful to pay taxes to Ceasar, or not? Should we pay them, or should we not?"

Now with that background, let us look at the text in question here. The Pharisees were a religious sect that considered themselves to be the real Jews, that is, those who were the true followers of God. This group made up many rules of piety to prove their purity and zeal for God. They also despised anyone who did not subscribe to their traditions (Matthew 15:2). Because of this, they would often be in a clash with Jesus because He did not think much of their traditions. In fact, He said that they placed their tradition above the word of God (v. 3-9). Therefore, instead of bringing people to God, their traditions only served to keep people from God.

The Herodians on the other hand, were those who were close political supporters of King Herod. They were in a sense, agents who tried to see to it that the people conform to the regulations of the government. It is important to note that the Herodians and the Pharisees were not friends, but they both shared the same agenda of getting rid of Jesus. So they combined and hatched a plan to trap Jesus in what He said since they were finding it difficult to prove that He did anything wrong. They insisted that they were going to get Him by any means necessary.

The leaders sent some Pharisees and some Herodians to get the job done. They asked Jesus, "Is it lawful to pay taxes to Caesar, or not?" (Mark 12:14). This was a very tricky situation. If Jesus said that they should pay taxes, then the crowd would be against Him. If he said that they should not pay taxes, then the king would be against Him. So, this was a serious dilemma politically. Either He would be destroyed by the crowd or by the crown. What Jesus did next should serve as a principle in dealing with political or any difficult issue. Jesus did not tell them what they wanted to hear, but He told them what they ought to hear.

Let's examine Jesus' response to these tricksters. Firstly, Jesus let them know that He was aware of their motive and plan. He also asked them to show Him the coin so that He could teach them a lesson (Mark 12:19). When they had brought the coin to Jesus, he asked them whose image and whose inscription was written on the coin. They cried out, "Caesar." So Jesus said, *Give to Caesar the things that belong to Caesar and give to God the things that belong to God.* This answer clearly tells us that we have a responsibility to give to the government what is their due. Paul in his letter to the Romans tells us that governments are set up by God and therefore, if we resist or rebel against government, we are rebelling against God (Romans 13:1-7). Of course, we should not obey a government that wants us to do things that are displeasing to God or are clearly against the teachings of Scripture. This is what caused the disciples in the early church to resist the powers that be at the time (Acts 4:10-21).

There is a very interesting point being made here in the text when Jesus sent for the coin. The coin of that day had the image of the emperor Tiberius Caesar. It also had an inscription which referred to him as god. So, Jesus was saying whatever is due to Caesar give it to him. What is it that was due to Caesar in this situation? Taxes. Jesus continued by stating that what is due to God must be given to Him. So we must not pay God our taxes and give the government our worship. Pay your taxes to the government but your worship is due to God because he alone is worthy of worship. Jesus was saying to them that they should give Caesar his money because his image is on it, and give God their life and their worship because His image is on them. We are created in the image and likeness of God (Genesis 1:27).

Finally, this passage should serve as a warning to people who come before Jesus with flattering words. It is very comforting when we understand that Jesus knows all about our troubles, but it is also sobering when we understand that He knows about all our pretense and hypocrisy. Jesus knows whether or not we are sincere. So let us be true so that when we worship Him, it is in spirit and in truth, for that's the kind of worshipper the Father seeks (John 4:23). So, give the government what is due to the government and to God what belongs to Him.

## Additional Questions to Ponder/Discuss

a. When is it fitting for us to disobey the government?
b. Has anyone ever tried to get you into trouble because you believe in God?
c. Why is it wrong for us to worship our leaders?
d. Why should we obey our leaders?
e. Since God's image is on you, who must you worship?

# 30.
# If I am your father, where is my honor? —Malachi 1:6

## No Lame Worship

"A son honors his father, and a servant his master. If I am a father where is my honor? And if I am a master where is my fear? Says the Lord of host to you, O priests, who despise my name. But you say how have we despised your name?" (Malachi 1:6)

God lays down the premise for His argument. It goes like this, a son honors his father and servants honor their Master, so God deserves honor as well because they claim that God is their Master and Father. In this context the people were treating God with disrespect and a lack of reverence. They offered lame sacrifices which they were not to offer (Leviticus 22:22). God was not pleased with their behavior. Therefore, he said that he would prefer that someone would close the temple doors (Malachi 1:10).

God makes the point that they have more respect for their governor than for Him because they would not offer spoiled meat to their Governor if they wanted his favor (Malachi 1:8). The Israelites did not understand why God was not pleased with what they were offering. They expected God to be happy for the fact that they came to the temple and that it did not matter what they gave. The issue here was not about the amount of offering, but the type of offering given. They were giving God their spoiled food with lame, sick and blind sheep (Malachi 1:7-8).

In Psalm 50:7-15 God told His people that He does not eat the flesh or drink the blood of animals. He was explaining to them that the whole world belongs to Him. So, when we see people today focused on the amount of money they give, as if it brings them closer to God, we know they are missing the message.

Many times preachers emphasize the portion of Scripture that says God loves a cheerful giver. It is true that God loves a cheerful giver. But the giving in Scripture is more about a person's heart than it is about the person's purse. The same text also states that one must give as he has committed in his heart (2Corinthians 9:6-7). The previous chapter in 2 Corinthians 8:1-5, makes it clear that what pleases God is not the amount of money we give but how we give. For example, the Macedonian Church was extremely poor and going through severe tests and afflictions, but they insisted on participating in helping the churches who were struggling to make ends meet.

Please note verse 5 which says that they first gave themselves to the Lord. The real issue today is not about Christians robbing God by not giving him their tithe, rather they are robbing God by not giving him their time, talent, treasure and their temple (which is their body) belongs to God. I want to make a point here which I believe is very important. **If we give all our money to God and keep ourselves from Him, we are still robbing God.** So can a person rob God? Yes! By withholding himself from God. Why is this true? Because the earth belongs to the Lord and everything in it (Psalm 24:1). If God is your Father, you need to give Him honor.

## Additional Questions to Ponder/Discuss

a. How is your worship to God now?
b. Do you show more respect and regard to your leaders than you do to God?
c. When you go to church do you spend more time texting than praising?
d. What is your primary reason for going to church?
e. How do you feel about the way worship is treated at your church?

# PART 8:

# DEALING WITH FORGIVENESS

# 31. How Many Times shall I forgive my brother when he sins against me? —Matthew 18:21

## Release Them, Set Yourself Free

"Then Peter came to Jesus and asked, "Lord, how many times shall I forgive my brother when he sins against me? Up to seven times? Jesus answered, "I tell you, not seven times but seventy-seven times" (Matthew 18:21, NIV).

The issue of forgiving others is one of the most challenging issues among all people and in all generations. As human beings we are far more welcoming to a discussion on receiving forgiveness than we are about giving forgiveness.

This is primarily because forgiveness is so hard when the pain is so deep. The more extreme the pain and suffering we endure, is the more difficult we find it to forgive those who hurt us. However, although it is difficult, it can be done with God's help. The Apostle Peter needed some clarity on the matter of forgiveness after hearing Jesus' teaching on the subject.

That brings us to the portion of Scripture we want to examine in Matthew 18:21 which says, "Then Peter came to Jesus and asked, "Lord, how many times shall I forgive my brother when he sins against me? Up to seven times?"

22 Jesus answered, "I tell you, not seven times, but seventy-seven times" (NIV)

Peter asked that question right after Jesus explained to them how they should deal with issues where they are sinned against. Jesus told them to deal with private offences privately. Go directly to the person to resolve the issue. If the issue is resolved, then leave it there; nobody else has to know. If it is not resolved, then get one or two other persons to help address the matter and to witness the situation. If that doesn't work, it must be taken to the church (Matthew 18:15-17). The context indicates this would apply only to offenses inside the Christian community. If the person remains rebellious and refuses to repent, he must be treated like an unbeliever. It does not mean he is now not saved; it simply means he is put out of the fellowship, with the hope that he comes to his senses and repents.

Now I will list seven pointers regarding forgiveness with the hope that it will get us to a place where we are more willing to forgive.

### 1. The person of forgiveness

In Matthew 6:12 Jesus taught his disciples to pray "forgive us our trespasses as we forgive those who trespass against us"

A little girl was reciting this prayer in class one day and she said "and forgive us our **trash passing** as we forgive those who trash pass against us". Now I know her version of the prayer is not quite accurate, but I think there is a nugget of truth in it. We can identify with the fact that people sometimes talk bad things that are not true about us. We need to forgive them for their trash passing against us.

God is the person of forgiveness who has given us an example to follow. We too become people empowered to truly forgive others from our hearts. Paul tells us that we should bear with each other and forgive each other as the Lord has forgiven us (Colossians 3:12-13; Ephesians 4:32). This truth is repeated in many other places in scripture to show that our forgiving of others is in light of God's forgiveness towards us.

### 2. The principle of forgiveness

The principle of forgiveness is basically releasing someone of their requirement to pay a debt. It means to let the person go free without demanding the payment of the debt. It is important to clarify what is meant and what is not being said. We are not implying that if you forgive someone, you must forget what they have done. If by 'forget' you mean erase from your memory, that is not how the Scripture uses 'forget'. For example, God forgave the people of Israel and said that he has removed their sins and will no longer remember them, but do you think that those things are removed from the mind of God? No! If you read carefully you realize that God sometimes reminded his people of how he forgave them. Therefore, He would have known what He forgave them of.

When God "forgets" our sins He is simply saying that He is not holding those sins against us anymore. Let us look at how the Apostle Paul used the word forgetting in Philippians 3:13-14. He told us that he has forgotten a number of things, but he just listed the things he claimed to forget. So what is Paul saying? He is doing the same thing God does when he "forgets" our sins.

Paul mentioned in verse 5-7 that he was "Circumcised on the eighth day, of the tribe of Benjamin, a Hebrew of Hebrews; as to the law, a Pharisee; as to zeal, a persecutor of the church; as to righteousness, under the law blameless. But whatever gain I had, I counted as loss for the sake of Christ." Paul listed his privileges, accolades and credentials which would make him significant before people. When he received Christ as Lord of his life, he counted those things as rubbish. Now he was still able to "list the rubbish", but he does not remember them with any significance. We do not count them anymore against the one who hurt us. So, when we say we forgive and forget all we mean is that we will not remember it against the person anymore.

Another thing we want to understand clearly is that there are different types of forgiveness. There is familial forgiveness, which is what Jesus was referring to in Matthew

6:12,14-15. This is not talking about salvation. If it were, millions of Christians would have gone to hell, and millions more would be going because many have died without forgiving someone. What Jesus is talking about is how to keep in fellowship with God. So when we refuse to forgive others, we have blocked the channel for our forgiveness. It is as we forgive those who trespass against us that we open the channel for our forgiveness.

There is also judicial forgiveness in Scripture. This kind of forgiveness is only applied in a transactional way, meaning you confess and repent and the other party forgives you. However, there are times when we need to give unilateral forgiveness. This is when we forgive without the offender repenting or asking for forgiveness. As difficult as it sounds, it is necessary for our personal healing and possible reconciliation. Sometimes the person who has wronged us has died or that person has now lost their mind and cannot hold a conversation; at other times the person may have moved away and there is no way of contacting them. If we are waiting for them to repent and ask for forgiveness, we will be waiting while hurting with no hope of healing.

## 3. The pain of forgiveness

Sometimes we ask ourselves, if forgiveness is such a good thing, why does it hurt so much to do it? Here is the difficult point in forgiveness—we normally do not like to feel pain. And when we have an attitude of forgiveness, we can set ourselves up for more pain. In fact, some people will seek to abuse you when you make yourself vulnerable through kindness and a willingness to forgive easily.

The option to not forgive is worse because we all need forgiveness at some point. We have hurt others and even hurt God. Therefore, the saying is true that when we refuse to forgive, it is like burning a bridge that we also need to cross. Someone else puts it this way. "Forgiveness is like setting a prisoner free and then realizing that the prisoner is me". This is crucial to understand because when we hold people hostage through unforgiveness, we only keep ourselves trapped in a prison that is locked on the inside. You have the keys to open the prison bars, release them and set yourself free. You see, the problem with unforgiveness is that it keeps us in prison and out of fellowship with God.

**4. The person who has been forgiven**

The unforgiving servant in our story in Matthew 18:21-35 was a forgiven servant. Here we want to look at *the Person who has been forgiven.* When the servant of the king was not able to pay what he owed, the King forgave him the debt. But when he found someone who owed him, he refused to show mercy. Instead, he choked the person and brought him to prison. When the King heard, he was angry and disappointed. The King threw that unforgiving servant into prison.

Jesus says to us that this is how the heavenly Father will treat us if we do not forgive others from our heart (v35).

Freely we have received, let us freely give. Acts 20:35 tells us, "It is more blessed to give than to receive," but some people only use this verse when they are talking about money, but this verse is not primarily about money, it is about giving. Giving includes offering mercy and forgiveness. In Matthew 5:7, Jesus says "Blessed are the merciful for they shall obtain mercy". So we need to stock up some mercy because we are going to need it.

**5. The privilege of forgiveness**

This is wonderful on both sides, whether you are the giver or the receiver. It is a privilege to offer forgiveness even though you have been offended. Scripture tells us that good sense makes someone slow to anger and it is his glory to overlook an offense (Proverbs 19:11). It is also wonderful to be set free from offenses, when you are released from your debt. This brings healing to a person's mind and body.

**6. The power of forgiveness.**

Forgiveness has a freeing effect, and a healing effect. It has the power to turn the worst of enemies into best friends. Let me give a caution here, I am not suggesting that all relationships where there is forgiveness there is also reconciliation, because they are not one and the same thing. There are persons who might have done real evil things to us or to our loved ones who are not trustworthy to be allowed into our space, nor would it be prudent to do so. What I am saying is that even though it is mandatory to forgive them, reconciliation is not always mandatory because it might mean putting yourself or your family in danger.

### 7. The purpose of forgiveness

We get a good picture of the purpose of forgiveness in the text before us. Notice what the King said at the end. "Should you not have mercy on your fellow servant as I have had mercy on you?" (v 33) Here is the crux of the matter, God wants to free people, who would then free people. He forgives us so we can be forgiving. He shows us mercy so we can be merciful. Forgiveness is not a feeling, so don't wait until you feel the feeling to do it. Forgiveness is an act of the will. In this story the man did not forgive, not because **he could not**, but because **he would not** (v 30).

As you reflect on the question Peter asked and the seven keys to forgiveness, do not stop the flow of grace in your life. Let us not keep ourselves in bondage by refusing to release those who hurt us. Let us release them and set ourselves free.

## Additional Questions to Ponder/Discuss

a. Why do people find it hard to forgive others?
b. Is there someone that you are bitter against even now?
c. Why did the servant refuse to forgive?

d. Do you believe that some people must not be forgiven?

e. Do you think that you deserve forgiveness?

# 32.

# Where are your accusers?

## —John 8:10

## Grace Others and It Will Come Back to You

One day while Jesus was in the temple teaching, some Scribes and Pharisees came to Him with a woman they claimed was caught in the act of adultery. They placed her in the midst of the people and sought to get their desire by trapping Jesus. Jesus, however, was too wise for those men. Let us look at how the story unfolded.

The Scribes, who were teachers of the law and also frequently involved in priestly duties, joined the Pharisees in an attempt to get Jesus to say something that could be used against Him. The Pharisees were a group of religious people who thought that they were the closest to God. They thought that they possessed a level of holiness which was superior to everyone else. This attitude caused them to be very self-righteous.

They also sought the praise and applause of people rather than the applause of God. John 8:3-6 says,

> And the Scribes and Pharisees brought a woman who had been caught in adultery, and placing her in the midst they said to Him, 'Teacher, this woman has been caught in the act of adultery, now in the law, Moses commands us to stone such women. So, what would you say?' This they said to test Him, that they might have some charge to bring against Him. Jesus bent down and wrote with His finger on the ground.

I want to first address the issue of Jesus writing on the ground with His finger. We must not put any significance to it or put any meaning to it. Nor should we apply it to the writing of the ten commandments by the finger of God. We must not read into the text what is not there. The Bible does not tell us what Jesus wrote or why He wrote it.

Jesus acted as if He did not hear them, but they persisted to try to get Him to answer them. These men were not seeking to uphold the law because the text already told us why they brought the woman and asked the question. Even though she was caught in adultery, they were only using her sin to accomplish their purpose. These Scribes and Pharisees were treacherous, disloyal and deceitful.

Look at how Jesus treated the situation, Firstly, Jesus exposed their hypocrisy and double standard. Did you notice that she was "caught in adultery" so where was the man? Did they let him go? Did he escape as they attempted to take him to Christ? Jesus in His wisdom said, "He that is without sin among you, let him first cast a stone at her" (John 5:8:7, KJV). After Jesus said that, they all walked away because they were all guilty of sin, which was evident in their plot and in their double standard and hypocrisy. If we are going to need forgiveness, we had better start learning to forgive. Grace is one of those treasures that the more you give it away, you are not any poorer, because it comes right back to you.

Jesus demonstrated love and compassion with wisdom. This is important to note because if Jesus had commanded them to stone her to death, He would be in trouble with the Roman government who was ruling at that time. Only Rome was allowed to perform capital punishment. This is why the Jews appealed that they could not crucify Jesus (John 18:31). If Jesus had just commanded them to let her go, He would be ridiculed by the religious leaders for not honoring the law of God which is written in Leviticus 2:10 and Deuteronomy 22:22, that such a woman be stoned to death.

Notice that Jesus did not condemn her nor did He condone her sin. Jesus said to her in verse 10-11, "Where are those thine accusers? Hath no man condemned thee? Neither do I condemn thee: Go and sin no more". Jesus, as the just judge in the situation, gave her correction and comfort. We need to follow Jesus' example and judge rightly and righteously.

Matthew 7: 1-5 tells us that we will be judged according to how we judge others. We need to do some self-evaluation as we seek to approach others about their sins. Jesus says, "Why do you see the speck that is in your brother's eye, but do not notice the log that is in your own eye (Matthew 7:3-5).

If we do not deal with ourselves first, we will not be of great help to those who really need it. People like when others are real with them, they don't want our camouflage. Galatians 6: 1-2 says, "Brothers, if anyone is caught in any transgression, you who are spiritual should restore him in a spirit of gentleness. Keep watch on yourself, lest you too be tempted. Bear one another's burdens, and so fulfil the law of Christ".

So, we must hunt them, but not to hurt them. We should hunt them so that we might help them. The text says, "You who are spiritual" should go and restore. Not you who are talented and gifted. It is a task for those who are demonstrating the fruit of the spirit in their lives. We must not be people who are like the Scribes and Pharisees, who think that they are above falling or failing in an area in their life. We must be loving, gentle, kind, patient, peaceful, faithful, forgiving and have self-control. We must be people who seek restoration instead of condemnation—a genuine goodness in heart with a pure motive. So let us seek to be confronters and comforters and not condemners and condoners, and exercise forgiveness.

## Additional Questions to Ponder/Discuss

a. Why is it so important to give grace and extend forgiveness to others?
b. How should we approach others who have fallen?
c. Why is it necessary to do self-evaluation first?
d. How does humility help in the rescue effort?
e. Who should be involved in the restoration process?

# PART 9:

# DEALING WITH TRUST AND ASSURANCE

# 33.
# Why have you come?
# —1 Samuel 17:28

## Confidence in the Deliverer

> Your servant has struck down both lions and bears, and this uncircumcised philistine shall be like one of them, for he has defied the armies of the living God. 37. And David said, "The Lord who delivered me from the paw of the lion and from the paw of the bear will deliver me from the hand of this philistine." And Saul said to David, "Go, and the Lord be with you" (1 Samuel 17:36-37).

The battle was set to take place between the Israelites and the Philistines. But the Israelites were very afraid because the champion of the Philistines was a giant. They didn't think that anyone on their team could match him. They saw no one big enough and no one who had the kind of experience in battle like he had. They were terrified, and no one wanted to go out on the battlefield.

It was at this time that a young boy named David came to the place and saw what was happening. He heard the Philistines mocking the Israelites and their God. A godly indignation rose up in David and he was compelled to do something. A great price was offered for any man who was able to defeat the giant. He would be given riches, the King's daughter in marriage and his family would live free from taxes in Israel. What a deal! Many would have loved those prizes but they were not willing to pay the price (1 Samuel 17:24-25).

David brought good news in troubled times. He told them that God is big enough, that He is strong enough, that He is the Lord of hosts (v45). The God of their armies had never lost a battle. Here is an important note; whenever you are about to do something significant for the Lord, look out for opposition. In 1 Samuel 17:28-29 it says that Eliab his eldest brother heard when he spoke to the men. And Eliab's anger was kindled against David, and he said "Why have you come down? And with whom have you left those few sheep in the wilderness? I know your presumption and the evil of your heart, for you have come down to see the battle." This means that the opposition can come from someone in your own family. David's brother came forward to accuse him of being a show-off, and of having a dirty heart. He accused David of being careless and irresponsible. But David kept his focus on the task at hand. David knew that he was there for a purpose and that purpose was to glorify God. Eliab thought that he only came into the trenches to watch but David was in the trenches to war with the enemy.

We all face giants of some kind in our lives; some physical, some emotional, some financial, and others spiritual. By giants, I mean a problem that is bigger than you, one that seems insurmountable. This passage gives us some tips on how to approach the situation. The point that jumps out from the pages is that we need to have a personal experience with God. David knew God for himself, he was not just repeating what others have told him about God (1 Samuel 17:34-36). Another thing that is crucial is trusting in and depending on God. David did not trust in his own abilities, but he trusted in God (v.37). Sometimes we can get carried away with our own status or stardom, but that is a dangerous place to be, when we believe we can do it without God. That's when we are most vulnerable in our battles.

If we are going to do well in the fight, we need to also remember what God has done for us in the past. This doesn't just encourage trust in God but also gratitude to God. David called to remembrance the wonderful things that God had done for him (v37). As we keep in mind what God has done for us in the past, it builds our courage to face other problems in the present or future (v 34-37). David's experiences in the past convinced him that giants surely do fall.

Remember that the battle belongs to the Lord. Here David tells us that God can save us without depending on our strength or weapons or skills (v 47). "Some trust in chariots and some in horses, but we will remember the name of our

God" (Psa.20:7). David did not depend on the strength of Saul's armor but on the strength of the Lord (vv. 38-39). He knew that Who he was going into the battlefield with was tried and proven. David was not trusting in his sling and stones to kill Goliath, rather he was trusting in the Rock of Ages to win the battle (v. 37, 45-47). Not once did David speak of his skills. He only spoke of his part in the battle by mentioning that God would give him the victory.

David was focused on working for the cause of the Lord and not for his own cause, and that is the reason why David went on the battlefield. He gave the glory to God for his victories, and we must do likewise. If you have something to do for God, don't watch the crowd just move out and do what God calls you to do. It may be that some will join when they see what God is doing through you. After David defeated Goliath, the rest of the army ran onto the battlefield to engage the enemy (v.52). If you have been on the sidelines just watching and not participating in the Lord's agenda, it's not too late to jump in.

I want to make an observation here that when we get involved in the Lord's business; when we honor His agenda, there is a reward to be received. The people of Israel were able to get their land and other things from the enemy (v. 52-53). The giant will fall as we walk right. Do what God tells us to do. Obedience is key to our march to victory. The giant will fall as we worship right, as we celebrate God, as we big up God, as we give God the glory.

Lastly, the giant will fall as we war right. Remember who the enemy is. Don't be like Eliab and fight against your family while staying on the sidelines. We are called to fight the good fight of faith. God will give us the victory but we have some fighting to do. Are you now on the battlefield for the Lord or are you on the sideline for your own interest? One of the areas that we need to get onto the battlefield is giving a defense for our faith. Peter says that we should, in our heart, regard the Lord as holy, always be prepared to give a defense or reason for our faith in God. However, he warns us to do it with gentleness and respect (1Peter 3:15-16).

He wants us to give reason and walk right so that we will not hinder the message of Christ. In Mark 12:30 we are told that we should love the Lord with all our heart and soul and mind and strength. We must conduct ourselves with wisdom and integrity, that we might know how to answer correctly. As we walk this path, our model of dignity and self-control will be a good attraction for Christ (Colossians 4:5-6). So, will you be a good soldier for the Lord today?

## Additional Questions to Ponder/Discuss

a. Why was David's brother so hostile towards him?
b. What was David's claim to fame?
c. Why do we need to remember who the enemy is?
d. What kinds of giants are you facing today?
e. Should we trust in our spiritual armor or in the power of God?

# 34.
# Who shall separate us from the love of Christ? —Romans 8:35-39

## The Strength of God's Love

Who shall separate us from the love of Christ? Shall tribulation, or distress, or persecution, or famine, or nakedness or sword? As it is written, "For your sake we are being killed all the day long; we are regarded as sheep to be slaughtered." No, in all these things we are more than conquerors through him who loved us. For I am sure that neither death nor life, nor things to come, nor powers... Nor height nor depth, nor anything else in all creation, will be able to separate us from the love of God in Christ Jesus our Lord. (Romans 8:35-39)

The passage before us has engendered many controversies because some people are glued to a particular tradition. They have a firm commitment to their tradition, so the issue is treated with much emotion. These discussions and debates often become hostile and bring more heat than light. Therefore, I ask you to lay aside your tradition for a moment and revisit the Scripture. It is important to note that when the question was asked in Romans 8 :35 by the Apostle Paul, he was not talking about our love for God but about God's love for us. So the question is, "Who can separate us from God's love for us."

Let's consider some evidence from Scripture to answer this question. Romans 8:1 tells us that there is now no condemnation to us who are in Christ. In verse 31 we see that there is no opposition because God is for us and in verse 35-39, we learned that nothing can separate us from Christ's love. Note that the reason why there is no opposition is not because no one is against us, but Paul is emphasizing that the One who is for us, which is God, is the only One who has the right to condemn us, and He is the one who justifies us. Therefore, if He is on our side no one can win against us (Romans 8:31-33).

Paul lists several categories of things that are not able to separate us from Christ's love, but when he could not think of another category he simply said, "Or any other created thing" Let's look at this list in verses 38-39. Neither death nor life nor Angels nor rulers, nor things present nor things to come, nor powers, nor height nor depth, nor anything else in all creation, will be able to separate us from the love of

God in Christ Jesus our Lord. Did you see that? Paul just put everything else in that category. That means nothing known or unknown can separate us from Christ's love. He is saying in case I have not mentioned something that you are thinking about, it is included in the category of all created things. I am aware that there are some objections to this view, but let me offer some more evidence to support this claim.

We are told by Jesus that He gives those who trust in Him, eternal life, and they shall never perish (John 10: 27- 29). He said that we are secure in the Father's hand and no one can snatch us. In John 5:24 it states clearly that Believers have been passed from spiritual death to spiritual life. John continues in chapter 6:39-40 where he says, "And this is the will of him who sent me, that I should lose nothing of all that he has given me, but raise it up on the last day." We learn later in Ephesians that we have been sealed by the Holy Spirit until the day of redemption (Ephesians 4:30). That was only an echo of what he already mentioned in Ephesians 1: 13-14 that we were sealed when we believe, and we have a guaranteed inheritance of which the Holy Spirit is the proof. Remember that we are saved by grace alone through faith alone and by Christ alone (Ephesians 2:8-9).

Therefore, it is not by works of righteousness which we have done but by his mercy He has saved us (Titus 3:5). No amount of good works caused us to gain salvation, nor can it cause us to retain it. I am asking you to go outside your tradition for a moment and revisit the Scripture. We are saved by grace through faith and that's how we live.

Colossians 2:6 says "Therefore as we have received Christ Jesus the Lord, so walk in him." So we are to live in grace by faith in Christ. Please don't get me wrong, I am not saying that our work doesn't matter, of course it does matter. Let's look at how our good works impact our relationship. Firstly, it impacts our intimacy with God and our maturing in Him (1 Corinthians 3:1-4). If we are obedient to Christ, we will mature in our faith. However, many of the believers at the Corinthian church were carnal and not growing in the Lord. Secondly, our works matter because we can be good witnesses for Christ and hopefully win people for His kingdom. When we have a godly witness or testimony people will be able to see our good works and glorify our Father in Heaven (Matthew 5:16).

One more reason is that our works will be judged and we will be rewarded by God for how we live. We will all stand before the Judgment Seat of Christ to give an account (2Corinthians 5:10). Here we will have the privilege of hearing our Lord say, "Well done good and faithful servant." We are told in Scripture that the person who is saved cannot practice sin (1John 3:9). This is important because earlier he said that if we say that we have no sin we deceive ourselves and we are calling God a liar (1 John 1:8-10). So we are definitely not sinless but we cannot continually live in sin. If someone claims to be a Christian but still living habitually in sin that person needs to examine himself to see if he is in the faith (2 Corinthians 13:5).

The Bible says in 2 Timothy 2:19 "But God's firm foundation stands, bearing this seal; The Lord knows those who are his." So he actually knows those who belong to Him. Not everyone who claims to be Christians knows Christ (Matthew 7: 21:23). Jesus says that the tares and wheat may look alike but he knows them differently (Matthew 13:27-30). The Believers who compromise their standard will suffer loss of their reward, but not their salvation. This is made abundantly clear in 1Corinthians 3:13-15. Some Christians are disciplined with sickness and even death because of their rebellious lifestyle (1Corinthians 11:30-32).

With this kind of evidence, I do believe good works matter, but not to save us or to seal us, because sealing is the role of the Holy Spirit (Ephesians 1:13-14; 4:30). The person who is living inconsistently will not have the kind of confidence he needs to enjoy his walk with Christ. King David and the prophet Moses were disciplined for their sins but none of us actually believe that they lost their salvation. I wonder if any expert knows just how many sins would make a born-again believer become unsaved again. What type of sin must the person commit?

What happens to the Christian if all her life she has been faithful to God but she told a lie just before a bus hit her and killed her on the spot? Should we take it that she is gone to hell because she did not confess that sin? For the millions of Christians who have died, did they all confess every sin before they met their death? We strongly doubt that they all did. Is our salvation based on our last action? If we really believe Christians who do certain sins have lost their salvation, why do we continue to preach to them since they will not be able to get saved all over again.

I want to list seven things for us to consider about eternal security that may convince us that nothing or no one can separate us from God's love. The first one is the plausibility of security. The issue here is whether or not the teaching on security contradicts other teachings in the Bible, it does not as far as I know. Not only is it possible and plausible, it is true. We have many supporting scriptures to suggest that the principle of security is clearly taught. This is a picture of how God, as owner of His property, puts His seal or mark on them to show that they belong to Him (Ephesians 1:13-14; 4:30). The promise of security is evident in John 10:27-30; John 5:24; John 6:39:40.

The Scripture gives the impression that we can take Jesus at His word. The person of security is Jesus. He makes it clear that we will be sealed and kept by the Holy Spirit and not by ourselves. The issue of our eternal security is not about our personal perseverance but about the Holy Spirit's preservation of those who belong to God (2Timothy 2:19; 1Peter 1:5; Philippians 1:6). The permanence of security speaks to the duration of the seal which is until the day of redemption (Ephesians 1:13-14; 4:30). This passage in Hebrews 10:14-18, shows the power of security: it is about the strength of the Savior and His salvation. It is not about the strength of the saint, because we are not strong enough to keep ourselves saved. The reason we stay safe is because there is no condemnation to those who are in Christ. The one who could oppose us and condemn us is God, and He is the one who is for us, the one who has justified us. We have an assurance in Christ and therefore having this hope we must live pure (1John 3:3).

## Additional Questions to Ponder/Discuss

a. Why do some people believe that a true Christian can lose her salvation?
b. What can separate us from God's love?
c. What role does the Holy Spirit play in keeping us saved?
d. How strong and consistent would a Christian need to be to keep herself saved?
e. What does Matthew 7:21-23 say about some who call Jesus Lord, Lord?

# 35.

# If a man dies, will he live again? —Job 14: 14

## The Hope of the Afterlife

"If a man dies, shall he live again? All the days of my service I would wait, till my renewal should come" (Job 14:14). Is there an afterlife? This is a question that has been asked by many people throughout history. It's a question that comes to our mind when we believe death is drawing near. Job was a servant of God who suffered tremendously but he remained faithful to God. Job also had questions about life and death. One of the questions asked by Job is before us today. He asked, "If a man dies, shall he live again."

He was basically asking if everything about our existence ends in death. There are many skeptics today who believe that when a person dies that is the end of their existence. They usually reject anything Supernatural because it cannot be tested in a lab. However, there are several passages in Scripture that tell us of an afterlife; by that I mean after this life has come to an end. Job was firmly convinced that even after his death he will live to see God in a new and different body. In Job 19: 26-27 Job says, "For I know that my Redeemer lives, and at the last he shall stand upon the earth. And after my skin has been destroyed, yet with my eyes I shall see God."

Daniel 12:2 states that people will be raised from the dead in the end, some will be raised to be with God and others will be raised and be separated from Him. This is a serious situation to consider since we must all give an account to God for what we have done in the body. We are told in 2 Corinthians 5:10 that all Christians will stand before God to give an account of their Deeds. The small and great will also stand before God to be judged for the works done in the body (Revelation 20:11-15). There is a very interesting passage of Scripture in Revelation 6:10, where the believers who were killed for the name of Christ, were asking God how long He is going to wait to avenge their death. That means they were conscious of who they are and of whose they are. They also have knowledge of their past experience because they knew what had happened to them and who did it.

Some false preachers in Corinth were trying to overthrow the believers' faith by telling them that there is no resurrection of the dead. Paul argued for the fact of resurrection of the dead by pointing to Jesus' resurrection. He argued that since Christ was raised from the dead there is a resurrection to look forward to (1 Corinthians 15:20). Paul asked, "Now if Christ is proclaimed as raised from the dead, how can some of you say that there is no resurrection of the dead" (1Corinthians 15:12).

Paul presented some logical arguments that if there is no resurrection, Christ is still dead, and if Christ is dead then all who were preaching that He rose from the dead are liars, and if it is a lie then you are still in your sins (1Corinthians 15:12-17). That would mean all those people who died while trusting in Christ for salvation have perished and life is empty and meaningless if we only have hope in this life (1 Corinthians 15: 18-19). Paul explained how the dead are raised and with what kind of body they come (1Corinthians 15:37). The body will be renewed to an imperishable body that cannot die again. We are not yet what we shall be, for we shall be like Jesus, having a body like his (1John 3:1-3). This is why we can shout like the Apostle Paul when he said "Oh death, where is your victory? O death, where is your sting?" (1 Corinthians 15:55)

We cannot hide from death or cheat death but by trusting in Jesus we can beat death. Paul exhorts the believers to commit themselves to God and comfort each other with this truth. Why would this truth comfort people? Because they will see their loved ones again. Heaven will be better than this. We will not be floating around on the clouds but living in the new Jerusalem. Words cannot even fully describe its beauty and splendor. We will finally be able to live with God in His heavenly kingdom brought down to a new earth.

You think I look good now, just wait until I meet Jesus. What a day that will be! Glory, Hallelujah! We will all be raised either to dwell with God for all eternity or to be separated from him, you have to choose. The day is coming when we will no longer need the sun to brighten our day, because The Son will be shining before us forever, hallelujah!

## Additional Questions to Ponder/Discuss

a. Do you think that your existence ends when you die?
b. Give two reasons why people are so afraid of death?
c. What does the Bible say about those who will be resurrected?
d. How will the dead be raised? And with what kind of body will they come?
e. How can we beat death?

# Conclusion

Throughout this book I have sought to give biblical answers to the questions asked throughout the Scriptures, all of which are still relevant today. In closing, I want to suggest some steps that you should take if you are to truly benefit from this book. Firstly, make it a priority to spend time with God in His word. Intimacy with Jesus supersedes any church activity we might do. Secondly, submit and surrender your desires to the Holy Spirit as you go into the word of God because He is the one who illuminates and reveals truth to your heart. Get rid of anything that will hinder that process.

Thirdly, put what you have learned into practice. Remember the old slogan, *if you don't use it, you will lose it.* There will be no transformation until there is application of the information we receive. This kind of growth is only possible if you seek to read the Bible often and apply its truths. Share with others the truth and principles you have learned and develop a greater passion for Scripture.

Discuss the questions in different fora eg. Social Media, Bible study groups, in your family devotions or reasoning with friends, especially young believers. Use it in youth meetings for example. Start conversations with the questions from this book and insights shared.

Finally, practice to ask questions of the passage you are reading. Find out who is speaking, to whom the passage is referring, what did it actually say, and where and when did it happen. These are very important investigative questions that will yield necessary information to understand the text. This is how you can get a better understanding and appreciation of Scripture because context is everything. Seek to test everything; hold on to what is good (1Thessalonians 5:21). Examine things and hold on to that which is true. Do your best to present yourself to God as one approved, a worker who has no need to be ashamed, rightly handling the word of truth (2Timothy 2:15).

# One Last Thing

## Bonus Chapter Gift

You've made it to the end of the book. Thank you for sticking with me! I have a gift for you. It's an additional chapter with three questions.

Go to http://bit.ly/D2ABonusChapter to complete a form to request the chapter.

Once submitted, you will receive an email with the PDF bonus chapter. The three questions are:

- Is there anything too hard for God? (Genesis 18:9-14)
- What are you doing here? (1 Kings 19:9)
- Did not the same One fashion us in the womb? (Job 31: 15 )

## Book Review

Don't forget to leave an honest review wherever you bought this book online. Book reviews are the lifeblood of authors. It is social proof. Thank you.

### Author Contact and Feedback

For consultation, feedback or speaking engagements, contact the author at robinsongarfield15@gmail.com .

# Acknowledgments

I want to thank the people who have helped in the completion of this project. This includes Ruth Taylor, for her editorial work, guidance and patience throughout the process. Hyacinth Peart, Kevin Llewellyn, Elaine Burris, Kamille Batchelor and Inez Small for proofreading the manuscript.

I also want to thank Delano Palmer, Dameon Black and David Pearson for interacting with the manuscript and endorsing it.

Finally, I wish to thank my publisher, Extra MILE Innovators, for the wonderful work they have done. This project could not be a success without them.

# About the Author

**Garfield Robinson** communicates the Scripture in a clear and concise manner, filled with conviction. His passion is teaching people how to understand the Scripture and to improve their spiritual intimacy with God. He has a gift of using simple and common examples to communicate complex truths. He has been a football player and a coach for many years, and he has applied some of his coaching techniques in his ministry. This he often does by creating a picture of what is happening in the text.

He is convinced that people have questions and they need someone to give some satisfying answers. He is confident that the Bible has relevant answers to help people today. This is the thesis of this dynamic book by this gifted Bible teacher and disciple maker.

Made in the USA
Columbia, SC
28 June 2021

40946908R00133